formatio

TRADITION. EXPERIENCE.
TRANSFORMATION.

Formatio books from InterVarsity Press follow the rich tradition of the church in the journey of spiritual formation. These books are not merely about being informed, but about being transformed by Christ and conformed to his image. Formatio stands in InterVarsity Press's evangelical publishing tradition by integrating God's Word with spiritual practice and by prompting readers to move from inward change to outward witness. InterVarsity Press uses the chambered nautilus for Formatio, a symbol of spiritual formation because of its continual spiral journey outward as it moves from its center. We believe that each of us is made with a deep desire to be in God's presence. Formatio books help us to fulfill our deepest desires and to become our true selves in light of God's grace.

SEEKING
GOD
TOGETHER

An Introduction to
Group Spiritual Direction

ALICE FRYLING

IVP Books

An imprint of InterVarsity Press
Downers Grove, Illinois

InterVarsity Press
P.O. Box 1400, Downers Grove, IL 60515-1426
World Wide Web: www.ivpress.com
E-mail: email@ivpress.com

InterVarsity Press® is the book-publishing division of InterVarsity Christian Fellowship/USA®, a student
movement active on campus at hundreds of universities, colleges and schools of nursing in the United States of
America, and a member movement of the International Fellowship of Evangelical Students. For information
about local and regional activities, write Public Relations Dept., InterVarsity Christian Fellowship/USA, 6400
Schroeder Rd., P.O. Box 7895, Madison, WI 53707-7895, or visit the IVCF website at <www.intervarsity.org>.

Scripture quotations, unless otherwise noted, are from the New Revised Standard Version of the Bible,
copyright 1989 by the Division of Christian Education of the National Council of the Churches of Christ in the
USA. Used by permission. All rights reserved.

Design: Cindy Kiple

Images: John Grant/Getty Images

ISBN 978-0-8308-3524-9

Printed in the United States of America ∞

 InterVarsity Press is committed to protecting the environment and to the responsible use of natural
resources. As a member of Green Press Initiative we use recycled paper whenever possible. To learn
more about the Green Press Initiative, visit <www.greenpressinitiative.org>.

Library of Congress Cataloging-in-Publication Data

Fryling, Alice.
  Seeking God together: an introduction to group spiritual direction
/ Alice Fryling.
     p. cm.
  Includes bibliographical references.
  ISBN 978-0-8308-3524-9 (pbk.: alk. paper)
  1. Church group work. 2. Spiritual direction—Christianity. 3.
Spiritual formation. 4. Discipling (Christianity) I. Title.
  BV652.2.F79 2008
  253.5'3—dc22

                                                              2008039556

P 24 23 22 21 20 19 18 17 16 15 14 13 12 11 10 9 8 7 6 5 4 3 2 1

Y 29 28 27 26 25 24 23 22 21 20 19 18 17 16 15 14 13 12 11 10 09

CONTENTS

Introduction 7

1 A First Look at Spiritual Direction. 9

2 Companions on the Journey 15

3 Group Spiritual Direction 25

4 The Power of Listening 35

5 Asking Life-Giving Questions 45

6 Exploring Thoughts and Feelings 55

7 Meditating on Scripture Together 65

8 Sin, Conviction and Confession 76

9 Sharing the Journey of Prayer 86

10 Temperament and How We Communicate 95

11 Discernment Among Friends 107

12 Troubleshooting Problems in Group Spiritual Direction. . . 119

13 Getting Started 126

Appendix 1: Suggested Format for Group Spiritual Direction . . 129

Appendix 2: Guided Meditations and Other Beginnings 130

Appendix 3: Discussion Guide for Seeking God Together 144

Suggested Reading 147

Notes 150

INTRODUCTION

I was introduced to spiritual direction well into my adult life. I had been involved in Christian ministry for decades. When I heard about spiritual direction, I felt as if I was seeing an old friend I had never met. Spiritual direction (this new but old friend) led me deeper into the love of God. Spiritual direction helped me experience more intimately the God of love. And spiritual direction equipped me to be in relationship with others where I could love as I was loved.

This book grows out of my own experience in both receiving and offering spiritual direction. My enthusiasm for what spiritual direction gives individuals and the people of God's church continues to grow. As I have watched people awaken to God's love in new and deeper ways, I have become more and more convinced that spiritual direction is an ancient tool which the church will continue to use for years to come.

But when I explored the possibilities for the ministry of spiritual direction within the church, I noticed two problems. First, sometimes individuals want to meet with a spiritual director and cannot find one. Second, for some people the step into personal spiritual direction is too big. The intimacy of meeting with one other person in a spiritual direction relationship may intimidate some who are unfamiliar with the practice. Discovering the richness of spiritual direction in small groups may be a good way for people to begin, as small groups are often a more familiar experience for many Christians. And of course, in small groups spiritual direction becomes more accessible to more people.

This book is designed to help people who are new to spiritual direction begin to understand how this ministry might work out with small groups of people. It is also designed for those who would like to start a ministry of spiritual direction in their church, as well as for individuals who desire to form a small group for spiritual direction on their own. I begin by describing and defining spiritual direction and then give practical help for those who want to facilitate or participate in group spiritual direction. I describe holy listening and suggest skills to help us listen more lovingly and attentively. In addition, we will look at some of the topics likely to be discussed in the spiritual direction encounter, specifically prayer, the Bible, temperament, sin and discernment. I also include practical helps for people leading spiritual direction groups.

The purpose of group spiritual direction is to provide a place where individuals can experience what it means to be listened to and loved by others, so that they can learn to listen more attentively to God in their daily lives and be used by God to spread God's grace and love throughout the world. God is using this ancient tool in life-giving ways in the twenty-first century. It is a privilege to participate in this experience.

1

A FIRST LOOK AT SPIRITUAL DIRECTION

I was very nervous the first time I went for spiritual direction. I had never done anything like this before. I wasn't even sure I knew what spiritual direction was. And I'd never met Ed, the spiritual director I found through a brochure someone gave me. We arranged to meet at a historic church near the campus of the University of Wisconsin. As I walked up the steps, I wondered how I had gotten myself into this.

Ed met me in the hallway of the church. We went into a large, Tudor-style parlor and sat in two wingback chairs. I thought, *This is like a scene from a novel.* Ed looked more like a college professor than the retired minister that he was. He even had a briefcase; he opened it and took out a doily and a small candle. *This seems very Roman Catholic. What if I don't know what to do?* As Ed lit the candle, he said "This is to remind us that we aren't alone." *Good thing. I guess he means that God is here with us.*

Then Ed introduced himself to me and asked me a few questions about myself. He read from the book of Isaiah: "Listen to me, O house of Jacob, all you who remain of the house of Israel, you whom I have upheld since you were conceived, and have carried since your birth. Even to your old age and gray hairs I am he, I am he who will sustain you. I have made you and I will carry you." *Maybe this won't be so bad after all.* Ed said he liked that passage. I said I did too. Then he asked me a question about my relationship with God. I don't remember the question or my answer. What I do remember is that when I had finished what I wanted to say, Ed just sat there, waiting and listening for more. *This is different,* I thought. People don't usually wait for me like that. They usually just talk more. But Ed waited and looked at me. *What I am supposed to do now?*

We sat in the quiet for several minutes. *I wonder if Jesus looked at people the way Ed is looking at me.* I don't remember who broke the silence, or what we said, but I do know that after every question Ed asked me, he waited. And waited. When I left that first spiritual direction session, I felt a deeper peace than I had experienced for a long, long time. *Perhaps,* I thought, *we really weren't alone in that room. God was indeed with us.*

I went home to the more familiar experiences of my life, to my own stresses and anxieties, and I realized that God was still with me. Before my meeting with Ed (and the Spirit of God), I certainly knew that God was with me. I knew that God had made me and sustained me. I knew that God promised peace. I knew all of that. But I had forgotten. I was like Jacob in the Old Testament. His life was full of very stressful circumstances. One night he had a dream where he met with God. When he woke up, he said, "Surely the LORD is in this place—and I did not know it" (Genesis 28:16). That's what my first spiritual direction session did for me. It reminded me that God was in my life. I had not been aware.

Awareness of God is one of the gifts of spiritual direction. The apostle Paul said in the New Testament that God is not far from each one of us. In fact, "in him we live and move and have our being"

(Acts 17:27, 28). But on my own I cannot always perceive God in my life. My spiritual eyes are clouded by the stresses, the fears and the unsolvable problems that are in the forefront of my awareness. Since that first meeting with Ed, I have been in dozens of spiritual direction sessions, with Ed and with others. As God listens to me, through my spiritual director and through silence, I begin again to listen to God.

The experience of spiritual direction has filled a longing in my soul. It has helped me be attentive to the whispers of the Holy Spirit in my life. Jesus promised that when he left this world, he would send the Holy Spirit. This Counselor and Spirit of truth lives in us (John 16:7-12). We no longer see Jesus physically, but with the eyes of our hearts we can see God's Spirit within. Spiritual direction helps us do that.

The Beginnings of Spiritual Direction

Spiritual direction is a way of companioning people as they seek to look closely, through the eyes of their hearts, at the guidance and transforming work of God in their lives. It's a practice that began in the early years of Christianity when people followed the desert mothers and fathers out to the wilderness to ask them how to know God. Over the years, spiritual direction has appeared in many faith traditions. It was kept alive in the Christian faith mainly through the Roman Catholic Church, but today the Protestant church is rediscovering it. People throughout the Christian church, including those of an evangelical orientation, are experiencing again the gifts that God gives to his people through the loving listening and the gentle guidance of spiritual directors. This gift is usually offered in the context of individual spiritual direction, but the potential for spiritual direction in small groups is a growing and promising expression of the ministry of spiritual companionship.

After my first meeting with Ed, I could not wait to tell my friends about it. My enthusiasm for spiritual direction led me to complete a certification program to become a spiritual director myself and meet regularly with individuals, to meet with my own spiritual director, and most recently to pursue spiritual direction in small groups. I continue to be amazed at the richness of this gift to the church, whether it is experienced individually or in groups.

GROUPS WHO LISTEN

A spiritual direction group is not your typical small group. It is not a study group or a place to simply find fellowship, although that happens. It is not a mission group, a committee or an accountability group. It is, first and foremost, a listening group. Just as Ed listened to me in personal spiritual direction, so members of the group listen, carefully and deeply, to one another. Just as Ed waited for me to say more, so members of the group wait for one another to share whatever they want to share at that time. And just as there was a lot of silence in the times I met with Ed, so there is a lot of silence in group spiritual direction.

Group spiritual direction provides a unique opportunity in the life of the church or community of believers. It is different from more typical conversations such as the superficial (but necessary) hi-how-are-you encounters or those that go a bit deeper but still require our best-dressed presentations. It's also different from our conversations and groups that revolve around meeting needs (casseroles for those who are sick, babysitting for those who are tired, mission work for those who are needy). It is different from teaching Bible studies, adult education classes, seminars and workshops. All of these things are very good things to do. But they do not provide the unique opportunity given in spiritual direction: the opportunity to be heard, to have someone listen to us as we describe the milestones, detours and questions of our own spiritual journeys.

Just as personal spiritual direction met a need deep within my soul, group spiritual direction provides a place where members of a small group can listen carefully to their own soul needs and to the needs of others. As each person is given an opportunity to talk about whatever they want to share, the group listens attentively, seeking together to hear the direction of God.

Participating in listening groups like this was a natural outgrowth of the wonder and peace I felt when Ed listened to me. I had read about group spiritual direction but never experienced it. When I tried it, I found that other people shared many of my own longings. We will get into the details of it later, but I will say here that the first meeting I had with friends was almost as scary as my first meeting for personal direction. I think all of us in the group were wondering what the experience would be like. Could we share personally and openly with each other? Would God really meet us there? Would this work? We could, God did, and yes, it worked.

Now, years later, I have learned that group spiritual direction was what many of these first friends were looking for. Julie said, "It was transformational because it was a place where I could talk about God and my relationship with Jesus. I discovered people like me— with yearnings and desires to grow spiritually. Those first meetings were especially exciting and fun for me." Other people have told me that it "fit where I was" and that "it met my need to move into a deeper relationship with God."

COMING HOME

Continuing to watch people participate in group spiritual direction over the years has been an amazing experience. Some people are quite shy about it. Others say that it is like a balm to the soul. Some people with a tenuous relationship with God seem to fall in love. Some know nothing about spiritual direction while others are looking for it. But for almost everyone, there is a sense of surrender to God's love, of "coming home" to God. This certainly describes my experience of both personal and group spiritual direction. I continue to be surprised by how familiar my "new" experiences of God's love are. The journey continues, but I always seem to be heading home.

This experience of returning to God's love has very practical ramifications. For example, early in my Christian life, before I had discovered spiritual direction, I tried to do everything anyone suggested should be done for growth or for service. My life was "directed," but it was directed by my perception of other people's expectations. As I began to let go of my need to please others at all times, I became more selective in what I did, but more driven. I was driven to prove to myself, to God and to others that I was worthy to be loved.

About the time I discovered spiritual direction, I was beginning to learn that trying to prove my worthiness to myself did not work any better than trying to prove my worthiness to other people. In my meetings with a spiritual director and in group direction, I began to experience what it means to have the Spirit of God direct my life. Over and over again, my experiences in spiritual direction remind me that I am already beloved by God. I do not need to prove that truth. The effect of spiritual direction in my own life is that I have become less active but more effective, and more passionate but less driven. The Holy Spirit directs my life with a gentle, caring touch. Over the years, my conversations in spiritual direction have continually reminded me that God is *always* waiting to extend grace and love to me in order for me to extend grace and love to others. This journey into personal and group spiritual direction is ongoing, fruitful and full of joy. I'm very glad I made that appointment with Ed.

2

COMPANIONS ON
THE JOURNEY

At the beginning of time, the first man lived with God in the Garden of Eden. Adam's relationship with God was meaningful and productive. It may have seemed as if life couldn't get any better. But God looked at Adam and said, "It is not good that the man should be alone" (Genesis 2:18). This has tremendous implications for those of us who want to move forward on the journey of spiritual growth. At the time God made that divine observation, Adam was perfect, created in his Maker's image. Sin had not yet tainted creation. But it was not good enough for Adam to live alone with God. He needed someone else. The poet John Milton said, "Loneliness is the first thing which God's eye named, not good." God knew that human beings needed human companionship.

Later in the Bible, we learn the magnitude of this need when we read that God actually "became flesh and lived among us" (John 1:14). God not only gave Adam a companion; the Creator God actually became a human companion in the person of Jesus in order to communicate divine love to all people. Jesus even told his disciples that he was their *friend* (John 15:15). God is not a cosmic reality outside of human relationship. God is a friend. Spiritual friendship, human and divine, is clearly God's idea and God's desire for us.

Most of us have friends. We have friends who are interested in the same things we are interested in. We have friends who share our faith perspectives. We have friends who help us. But in my mind, the best kind of friends are "soul friends." These are people with whom I can be forthcoming and honest about my own soul. In return, they reflect God's love for me in their words, their attitudes and their actions. These are friends who "enflesh" God for me. God loves me and nourishes my soul through these friends. My own spiritual director is one of my soul friends.

THE NATURE OF OUR SOULS

Before we look at soul friendship, we need to look briefly at the nature of our souls. The soul is more than the sum total of the mind, heart, spirit and body. My soul is my inner essence, my spirit, the core of my will and my desires. It is almost impossible to describe the soul in words, limited as we are by the semantics of language. Our souls are not separate parts of us, something we "have." Rather, the Bible speaks of the "soul" in language that reminds us to be attentive to this part of *who we are*. Jesus said, "You shall love the Lord your God with all your heart, and with all your soul, and with all your mind" (Matthew 22:37). Does this mean that our souls are separate from our hearts and our minds? Not really. Nor, as we will see later, are our hearts and minds separate from one another. Gerald May, a well-known psychiatrist and spiritual director, says that the soul "reflects the essence of one's existence. . . . It is manifested through, rather than divorced from, body, mind, or any other facet of one's being."

The Bible also speaks of the soul in terms of feelings and needs. Job's soul felt bitterness (Job 3:20). David's soul felt thirsty and parched (Psalm 143:6), as well as "terror" (Psalm 6:3). Jesus offered to give his disciples "rest" for their souls (Matthew 11:29). It is to the needs of our souls that spiritual direction speaks.

Because our soul is rooted in our unconscious, we don't always pay attention to, or even know, what it needs. In his book *The Dark Night of the Soul,* May notes that St. Teresa, John of the Cross and Brother Lawrence all "had a profound appreciation that there is an active life of the soul that goes on beneath our awareness." My soul is very private. It's so deep within me that others do not easily acknowledge it. Sometimes I'm so busy and preoccupied that I ignore my soul myself. Other times my soul cries out to me.

My soul friends help me listen to my soul. The "soul is not a separate part or aspect of a person, but rather what you see when you look at a person with spiritual eyes." Soul friends look at us with spiritual eyes and help us respond to our own souls. Spiritual direction is sometimes called soul friendship because it is a relationship where my soul speaks, listens and receives. But unlike other soul friendships, in the spiritual direction relationship the focus is intentionally on one person. One person is saying to another, "I would like you to accompany me on my spiritual journey." The purpose of this friendship is not that one person *directs* the other but that the spiritual director is a *companion* to the other. In other words, the spiritual director is not really the director. God is the director. Some people even prefer to call this ministry "spiritual companionship." I use the term *spiritual direction* (and *director* and *directee*) to keep this relationship rooted in its rich historical heritage, but whatever it's called, it is a relationship where two people meet together to seek God's direction, focusing on one of their lives.

This book is about how to find soul friendship through *group* spiritual direction. But first I will look at spiritual direction in its earliest form—where individuals meet one on one—and describe this relationship between individuals from my own perspective, both as a directee and as a director. Then in the next chapter I will look at the variety of ways people can meet in small groups for spiritual direction.

SOUL SHYNESS

I have been in spiritual direction as a directee for twelve years. And I have found out that I am a shy directee. When I first met with Ed, I was quite nervous. I didn't know what to expect. I wasn't sure I would like it, and I didn't know if Ed would like me. Now, years later, I'm still a little nervous when I meet with my spiritual director. As I drive west on Route 88 to my appointment, I wonder if she will think I'm doing a good job with my spiritual life. I know in my head that spiritual direction is not about seeking approval, but the temptation to do that is still with me. The truth is that, even though I'm getting used to it, I still feel a little anxious.

Not everyone feels anxious the way I do, of course. But most of us feel a little shy when it comes to talking about what's going on in our souls. Parker Palmer said, "the soul is like a wild animal . . . it seeks safety in the dense underbrush, especially when other people are around." Even Adam and Eve, the first man and his God-given companion, went into hiding when they heard God walking nearby, afraid he'd see the fresh sin in their souls (Genesis 3:8). My soul is continually tempted to hide, sometimes out of shyness, sometimes because of fear and sometimes because I just don't want to deal with the issues my soul is facing.

But after years of being in spiritual direction, I've discovered that it's the safest and most affirming of relationships. It's the place where, like Job, I can admit bitterness, and like David, I can acknowledge terror. I can say that my life feels parched and that I long for God. It is a place where I can hear Jesus' invitation to rest and be quiet. My relationship with my spiritual director is safe and affirming, not just because she's a mature Christian, but because Jesus lives in her

(Galatians 2:20) and Jesus loves and affirms me through her. Over the years I have come to see this soul friendship as a place where I can experience the companionship of God and hear the whispers of the Spirit.

WATCHING GOD AT WORK

In the spiritual direction relationship, the director is really listening in to an ongoing conversation between the directee and God. The Spirit has been at work in the directee's life before the direction session and will continue to be at work after the meeting is over. The most important part of a spiritual direction conversation is not what is said between the spiritual director and the directee. The most important part is what goes on between the directee and the Spirit of God. When I am the director, I often have the sense that I'm eavesdropping on someone else's conversation. Sometimes I'm surprised by what my friend hears. But what I hear in their conversation almost always resonates with what Scripture says about the truth and grace of God.

Margaret Guenther, author of *Holy Listening,* calls spiritual directors "midwives for the soul." The spiritual director is both as important and as unimportant as a midwife is to the birth of a baby. The midwife is important. He or she has seen many births and can provide helpful advice and guidance, but the baby does not belong to the midwife. And the midwife is not the one experiencing the pains of labor and delivery. The midwife is there to encourage, give some direction, and provide an environment where the birth is safe and protected. As we are born again (and again and again), we need someone in the delivery room to help us.

Using another medical analogy, Tilden Edwards in *Spiritual Friend* compares a spiritual director to a doctor:

Being a spiritual friend is being the physician of a wounded soul. And what does a physician do when someone comes with a bleeding wound? Three things: He or she cleanses the wound, aligns the sundered parts, and gives it rest. That's all. The physician does *not* heal. He or she provides an *environment* for the dominant natural process of healing to take its course.

In spiritual direction, the director helps others notice God in the most ordinary life circumstances, and provides an environment where spiritual healing can take place.

WHAT DOES A SPIRITUAL DIRECTOR DO?

What, then, does a spiritual director actually do? First and foremost, the director *listens*. To listen to another person in a way that helps that person hear the grace and truth of God is one of the greatest gifts we can give. Loving listening is active and engaged. It is more about offering questions than giving answers. In the spiritual direction relationship the focus is on the directee's relationship with God. This does not mean that we talk only about prayer or church or reading the Bible. Rather, we talk about everyday life—jobs, family, health, houses and desires. In spiritual direction we come back again and again to the question "Where is God in this?" Even more, we allow for times of silence so that the directee can actually notice God's presence in whatever they're experiencing. Veteran spiritual directors William A. Barry and William J. Connolly say that "the focus of this kind of spiritual direction is the relationship itself between God and the person. The person is helped not so much to understand that relationship better, but to engage in it, to enter into dialogue with God."

The spiritual director *welcomes* the directee into God's presence. Or more accurately, the spiritual director reminds the directee that God is already present, even in the most stressful experience of life. Sometimes people don't notice God's presence out of fear. This is probably not intentional or even conscious; all people are tempted, like Adam and Eve, to hide from God. We may, for example, hide because we consciously or unconsciously think we are not worthy to be in God's presence. We may hide because we think God is mad at us. We may hide in our attempts to only let our best self show. We may even hide behind our talents and gifts.

Thomas Merton, another veteran spiritual director, observed:

> The whole purpose of spiritual direction is to penetrate beneath the surface of a man's life, to get behind the façade of conventional gestures and attitudes which he presents to the world, and to bring out his inner spiritual freedom, his inmost truth, which is what we call the likeness of Christ in his soul. This is entirely a supernatural thing.

It takes a great deal of courage to come out from behind the "façade of conventional gestures and attitudes." This means that the environment of spiritual direction must be very welcoming, not judgmental, even of the hiding places. Remembering that the soul, like a wild animal, is shy, "we know that the last thing we should do is go crashing through the woods yelling for it to come out." Rather, in spiritual direction, we welcome whatever part of the soul chooses to reveal itself. We welcome it in love.

SAFE AND REAL

The spiritual direction relationship is a safe place, a place where we don't need to fear condemnation. Jesus told the disciples that he would ask the Father to give them a counselor, or advocate, who would be with them forever (John 14:16). The thought that God is my advocate is hard for me to remember. Like many people, I often think of God as an adversary. Because we know our inclinations toward sin, we may assume that God thinks of us only in terms of anger and punishment. We might express our fear of God in our fear

of other people, saying to ourselves, "If God or anyone else knew
what I really think and feel, then I would be doomed for sure!" Spiritual direction is a place to set aside those fears and be present with
God, knowing that the spiritual director, like the Holy Spirit, is our
advocate. The apostle John wrote that "God did not send the Son
into the world to condemn the world" (John 3:17). One of the greatest gifts of spiritual direction is that it provides a place where we
are not condemned but loved. Sometimes in spiritual direction conversations, we recognize truths about ourselves that we don't like.
But this truth, rather than accusing us, may set us free. A spiritual
director reminds us that God is indeed on our side.

The environment of spiritual direction, then, is affirming and encouraging, but it is also a place of authenticity. In spiritual direction,
we look at the truth of our present situation and experience. The
question asked is not "What *should* be happening in my life?" but
"What *is* happening in my life?" We look for God *here, now,* because
the place where we are in our lives is the place where we find God.
Our souls, our lives, are the dwelling place of God. We are God's
temple (2 Corinthians 6:16). God names himself the "I AM" (Exodus
3:14)—not the I-will-be, the I-was, the I-could-be, but the I-*am*. The
present moment, the present set of circumstances, the present relationships in our lives—this is where God lives. This is where God
meets us and gives us life. This is where spiritual direction occurs.

TRANSFORMATIONAL DIALOGUE

What happens, then, in this welcoming, safe, authentic place? What
kinds of conversations take place? We will look first at an individual
spiritual direction session, and then in the next chapter we will discuss what takes place during group spiritual direction.

A spiritual direction session often starts with silence, prayer or
Scripture. This time provides a buffer between all the activities
preceding the session and the attentive quiet necessary for listen-

ing to the Spirit of God. Then the director may ask a very general question, such as "How *are* you?" The directee may choose to bring up recent life events or be more specific in what they want to discuss. Either way, the conversation begins with the directee talking for several minutes about his or her own life, relationships or spiritual journey. The director might then invite the person to talk more about something, asking something like, "Could you say a little more about_____?" Or if the conversation is a rambling one, the director may look for themes or connections between the events or relationships, and respond with something similar to "It sounds like you felt _____ [helpless, angry, fulfilled, excited] a lot lately." If the directee resonates with that theme or word, they may talk more about what it means. If not, the directee may add a corrective to explain more clearly what he or she has been experiencing. Either way, together they move deeper into the directee's experience.

At some point, after a lot of listening, the director will perhaps ask, "What do you think God feels [or thinks or is doing] in you as you experience this situation or relationship?" Or, "Do you sense any gentle nudges from God in this?" Or, "How do you think God is inviting you to respond to this?" Sometimes the director may also gently introduce a passage of Scripture that seems relevant. And often, with the permission of the directee, the director closes in prayer.

All of this takes time—and some of the spiritual direction time is spent being silent. This can be hard for both director and directee, as they may want to keep talking. When I'm the directee, for example, I might avoid silence by talking on and on, defending myself or overdescribing a situation. When I'm the director, I may want to explain my understanding of what this conversation is about, make suggestions or give some answers. But silence in the direction session can become a resting place where God's Spirit whispers to our souls.

Spiritual direction is about transformational dialogue with God, not just an exchange of information between director and directee.

When the session is over, there may be a sense of joy and release for the directee. Other times it might feel more like they're stopping in the middle of an ongoing conversation with God. Sometimes the questions are answered. Other times they are not. But almost always, there is a deep sense of having been in the presence of God.

3

GROUP SPIRITUAL
DIRECTION

My own experience with group spiritual direction began a number of years ago when my husband and I moved from Wisconsin to Illinois. At that time I was in training as a spiritual director—something I happened to mention to the pastor of one of the churches we visited in our new community. He reached out, shook my hand with enthusiasm and said, "We have been *praying* for someone like you in our congregation." I suspected we might have found our new church home.

After we had been members of the church for a few months, the same pastor asked me to introduce spiritual direction to some of the people in the congregation. We decided to hold classes titled "An Introduction to Spiritual Direction" on several evenings, and the pastor sent out letters to people he thought would be interested. The morning after the letters were mailed, I had a serious case of cold feet. Who did I think I was? How could I do justice to this deep and wonderful ministry? What if no one came? *Actually,* I thought, *that might not be a bad idea.* So I prayed, quite literally, "God, maybe this whole thing should be canceled. If no one comes, we could do that. And I promise I won't take it personally." But the night of the first meeting about fifteen people showed up. They became the core of a thriving ministry of spiritual direction in our church. Dozens of people have participated in this ministry, a number of people have completed spiritual direction training programs, and many individuals are receiving personal spiritual direction. My cold-feet prayer is among those in my life that I'm glad God didn't answer as I expected.

One outcome of the class was that we began offering group spiritual direction in our church. We offered sessions which met for six weeks and invited new people to join each semester. These groups introduced more and more people to spiritual direction and facilitated spiritual growth in many, many lives.

WHAT HAPPENS IN GROUP SPIRITUAL DIRECTION?
Group spiritual direction is very similar to individual direction. A small group of people meet together to provide spiritual direction for each other. Members of the group are given the opportunity, one at a time, to be the directee, and the group responds prayerfully to whatever the directee chooses to present.

The format is simple. The group starts with a time of silence or a short meditation. After that the group invites one person to talk for five or ten minutes about whatever they'd like. Then there is another time of prayerful silence. Out of the silence, the group begins to ask questions, responding to whatever the directee is presenting. (We will get to the how-tos of this time of presentation and response in later chapters.) At the close of the person's presentation and the group's response, there is another time of prayerful silence during which each person in the group prays silently for the individual who presented. The group may choose to allow time for two people to present in one session, but in any case, over the course of several months, everyone will have the opportunity to be the directee.

The purpose of these groups is not counseling or therapy. Nor are they intended to be places where we can engage in aimless, self-absorbed conversations. The purpose of spiritual direction groups is *formation*. Spiritual formation is "a process of being conformed to the image of Christ for the sake of others." The intentional goal of group spiritual direction is to help each participant become more aware of God in their lives, *for the sake of others*. In other words, it leads to an awakening of the soul. This awakening then leads to a life which is purposeful and intentional. Group spiritual direction helps individuals grow in their faith, love others more fully and participate in the mission of the church more effectively.

LEADERSHIP OF THE GROUP

A group like this, which invites people to share their own spiritual journeys, be personal and authentic, and seek transformation for the sake of others, is very unusual. You won't hear the average after-dinner conversation when they meet. For this reason, spiritual direction groups need informed facilitators to lead, ideally people who have been trained as spiritual directors.

There are many excellent two-year programs around the country for training people gifted in spiritual direction. I cannot overstate my appreciation for the spiritual enrichment and practical benefits of the training program I attended. These programs are to spiritual directors what music academies are to musicians. If someone is gifted in violin, for instance, but never takes lessons, that person will probably not play well. But if someone is not gifted to play music on the violin, all the lessons in the world will not make a musician out of him. In a similar way, offering spiritual direction well means that the director has been given gifts from God to do this. But without training, these gifts may be less focused and less effective. So it's best to have the leaders in group spiritual direction be trained spiritual directors.

This, however, is not always possible. Spiritual direction is a ministry that's just being rediscovered in the Protestant church. Most churches don't have people who have already been through spiritual direction training programs. Yet people are seeing the benefits of spiritual direction and looking for ways to engage in the experience. When this is the case, group spiritual direction can be especially valuable, and it can be effective even without a trained spiritual director. One way to begin is to have a study group about spiritual direction so that everyone understands how unique, and yet how familiar, spiritual direction can be. (Spending a few weeks discussing this book might lay a good foundation. A study guide follows in appendix three.)

Whether you have a trained spiritual director in your church or not, what is essential is for each individual in the group to be committed to the spiritual direction process, and for someone who has proven skills in group leadership to be given the responsibility to facilitate the group process.

After the facilitator guides the group through the time of silence, he or she invites the assigned presenter to share from their life. Sometimes this means that the facilitator needs to encourage the presenter with a few open questions. Other times the facilitator needs to gently keep the presenter on track and within the time frame. The facilitator also needs to provide leadership for the group in their response, encouraging questions and discouraging advice. The job of facilitating group spiritual direction is not an easy one, but if the group shares the leader's commitment to the process, it works well.

In some groups, the facilitator also takes a turn as presenter. When that happens, he or she asks someone else to facilitate that session. In other groups, the facilitator is there only as a director and does not take a turn as directee. This is usually the case when the facilitator is a trained spiritual director.

The Essentials

Several ingredients are essential for group spiritual direction. *Absolute confidentiality* is on the top of the list. The group will be a place where personal soul-work happens. This kind of intimacy requires the confidence that nothing shared in the group will be shared outside the group. It is a good idea to reiterate the group's commitment to confidentiality from time to time.

Regular attendance is another essential ingredient. Group members need to commit to coming to each meeting if at all possible. Sporadic attendance is not an option if the group is to establish the trust and camaraderie necessary for authentic personal sharing.

It's also a good idea to schedule *brief times of evaluation* for the group. Usually groups make a commitment to meet biweekly or once a month for three to six months, but some groups meet for years. Whatever the initial commitment, be sure to set aside occasional times for people to comment on how they feel the group is doing.

Models for Group Spiritual Direction

Groups meeting for spiritual direction come in many shapes and sizes. Not all spiritual direction groups happen within a church setting. Some groups are defined by church membership or attendance, but other groups are made up of friends from several churches. Some groups are crossgenerational, some are age-specific. Some are made up of men and women, some are just one or the other. There are several models that can be followed for group direction.

Church groups. Churches are finding that group spiritual direction is a good way to introduce people to spiritual direction itself, providing an opportunity for them to begin experiencing this way of relating to others and to God. As I mentioned, in our church people had the chance to join spiritual direction groups each semester. The groups met every other week; at the first meeting of each season, I gave a brief introduction to spiritual direction so newcomers would

feel welcome. We met as a plenary group for the opening time of
silence, which usually included a brief meditation. Then we divided
into small groups, which stayed the same during each semester.
Usually each person had the opportunity to present as the directee
at least once.

If spiritual direction is new to the church, these groups might end
up being a little less personal than individual spiritual direction.
They may not be model-perfect. But they provide a good place to
begin. For some people, talking about their own spiritual journeys is
a very new experience. Listening to others attentively and quietly as
they also listen to the Spirit of God may also be a new experience. In
fact, this kind of conversation is so unusual that groups might seem
cautious, like a child learning to walk. As people become more and
more familiar with the group spiritual direction process, however,
the interaction in the groups becomes more personal, quieter and
more reflective. But even groups that are just beginning can introduce participants to a way of relating to God and each other that is
transforming and life-giving.

A group of friends. I have been meeting with a group of friends for
seven years. We call our group a *lectio* group because we are reading
very, very slowly through the Gospel of Luke. We're each committed
to reading the assigned verses (usually only a paragraph or two) and
asking ourselves the following questions: What stands out to me in
this paragraph? How does this truth or observation apply to my life
right now? And what is the invitation from God to me in these verses?
(A fuller description of *lectio divina* follows in chapter seven.)

When we meet, we allow each person as much time as she'd like
to share the answers to the questions and to present anything she
wants to from her life. As a group, we then interact with each person
in a spiritual direction style. Our sessions last for about two hours,
and because our group is small, everyone has a chance to present.
Though we don't call ourselves a spiritual direction group, we func-

tion in a spiritual direction manner. We have accompanied each other through many seasons of life, helping each other see God's loving work in our lives.

Groups led by a spiritual director. Groups are often facilitated and coordinated by spiritual directors. In this situation, the people in the group may not know each other beforehand. They are gathered together by the spiritual director and usually pay the director for the sessions. These groups work well because they meet together only for spiritual direction and are often very focused, much like individual spiritual direction.

A two-person group. Another creative way to experience spiritual direction is to meet with one other person and take turns being the director and the directee. Some people who choose this model meet for two hours, giving each person one hour to be the presenter. Other people decide to have one person function as the directee for three months, and then switch roles for the next three months.

Groups of young people. Young people are particularly inclined to process things with their friends, so group spiritual direction is a good fit. They may not, however, have the maturity and life experiences to function effectively in the traditional model of spiritual direction. Those who have offered spiritual direction to younger people report that they often need to be a little more directive than they are with adults.

That said, I asked several spiritual director friends about their experiences in group spiritual direction with high schoolers and people in their twenties. They all said that the model of group spiritual direction is an excellent one for students and young adults. One director told me, "The students already were sharing openly about their experiences with each other as friends. I just helped them bring these experiences before the Lord, and process them prayerfully." In one group a young woman found a place to talk about her struggles with depression. Another teenager admitted the fear that God was angry with her, because she thought she wasn't a "good enough Christian." Not surprisingly, groups of young people also talked about relationships—relationships with parents, siblings, friends and the opposite sex.

The qualities of leadership that are important in offering group direction to young people are similar to those for leading groups of older people. But one spiritual director emphasized the special need for "openness and genuineness about my own life, and unconditional love" for the students. With this kind of authentic, loving leadership, spiritual direction groups can be foundational and transformational for young people.

THE FRUIT OF SPIRITUAL DIRECTION

The fruit of both group and individual spiritual direction is life-giving. Tara said that when she first began in spiritual direction, she thought, *What a wonderful luxury, to spend time each month just on my journey, my issues, examining my relationship with God.* It wasn't long, however, before I felt like spiritual direction was no longer a luxury but a necessity." Someone else said that spiritual direction "helps me refocus my attention on what God is doing and the evidence of that in my life. It helps me to recall the main events over the past month, to bring them into focus and see where God has been at work." Speaking specifically about group spiritual direction, Erin told me, "I never had a safe place to talk like that—to be affirmed in my relationship with God."

I asked my friend Linnea to tell me about one of her experiences in group spiritual direction. She said that the night it was her turn to present as directee she decided to talk about her job situation. She is a consultant who takes on projects with different companies for various lengths of time, usually for one or two years. The job she was describing had lasted four years. During that time she had become very close to her team members as they worked through the problems of their particular project. Now that the project was over, Linnea felt the loss of those people and the company where she had been consulting.

In telling me about her time as directee in her group spiritual direction session, she said, "There were four people in the group when I presented. After I talked and we had a time of silence, one person in the group remembered the passage of Scripture where Jesus looked for one lost sheep. She suggested that I might be feeling lost and that Jesus might be looking for me. This prompted the next person to ask some relevant questions about my feelings of loss. I found that I was able to talk more deeply about the loss of companionship I felt." The group continued to support Linnea, focusing on the experience of grief. She said afterward, "It was a wake-up call to me because I always thought grieving was for someone who had died. I never thought of grieving as related to losing something. When I accepted this, I could walk through my experience of grief with acceptance and love. The whole process was not one person's feedback but the result of everyone in the group building upon each other's experience." This was clearly a memorable time for Linnea, one where she felt loved by several friends, enriched by their perspectives and supported by their caring attentiveness.

Offering the opportunity for people to gather in groups for spiritual direction is offering them the wonderful experience of focusing attention on their ever-growing relationship with God, in whatever life situations they're facing. Jesus said that we must be "born again"; spiritual direction is about noticing that birth, which happens on a daily basis. Each day Jesus is born in us. Just as the wise men traveled together to find Jesus in the manger, so we travel together to find Jesus born in our souls. When we meet together, whether as a group, as twosomes or as individuals in spiritual direction, we give each other the gift of listening in the name of Jesus. This kind of loving listening bears fruit in our own lives, in our fellowship with those we love and in our church communities.

4

THE POWER OF LISTENING

𝕯

The book of Job in the Old Testament is a story of a man who lost almost everything—his children, his house, his possessions and his health. Early in the book we read about three friends who came to support him. If I make an anachronistic leap in my mind, I can imagine these four men sitting around in a circle, looking very much like a spiritual direction group. Job was the directee, and his friends were offering him group direction. They didn't do a very good job.

Before we look at what these friends did wrong, notice what they did right. They were intentional. They went to some effort just to show up. They managed to sit with Job for *seven* days and *seven* nights, without saying a word (Job 2:13). I don't know if I could have done that. Apart from the grace of God, I would have certainly spoken up and would have justified my interference with the silence in any number of ways. Some of the "reasons" I would have had probably reflect the mistakes that Job's friends made.

"HERE IS WHAT I THINK."

Eliphaz was the first friend who could not resist speaking. "If one ventures a word with you," he said to Job, "will you be offended? /

But who can keep from speaking?" (Job 4:2). Apparently not Eliphaz. He went on to "comfort" Job with his own thoughts about Job's circumstances, implying that his own observations could relieve Job of his suffering.

As I have seen . . . (Job 4:8)

Now a word came . . . to me . . . (Job 4:12)

I have seen . . . (Job 5:3)

As for me, I would . . . (Job 5:8)

Then he capped it all off with this insensitive comment to his friend Job: "See, we have searched this out; it is true. / Hear, and know it for yourself" (Job 5:27). In other words, "Here is what *we* think. Now apply that to your situation."

I can't be too hard on Eliphaz. I have made his mistakes many times. I want to help. I want to comfort. The first thing that often comes to mind is what has been helpful and comforting to me, so I speak too quickly from my own experience and my own observations. I have also been on the receiving end of Eliphaz-style comfort. When our beautiful granddaughter was born with Down syndrome, many people tried to "comfort" me with a truth or a promise, "a word from the Lord." While I appreciated their intent, they did not really understand my own feelings at the time, which were mysteriously mixed and complex. I heard many things that were true, but often these comments didn't speak to me where I was at that time. My experience reminded me that in spiritual direction, group and individual, we need to carefully restrain ourselves from giving our own perspective on someone else's experience.

"WHAT DID YOU DO TO DESERVE THIS?"

The next to speak of Job's three friends was Bildad. Quite frankly, I think Bildad blew it from the start. "How long will you [Job] say such things? / Your words are a blustering wind" (Job 8:2 NIV). If I am in a very difficult situation, doing my best to keep my faith, I don't want someone to accuse me of speaking like a blustering wind! Bildad said that Job must have done something wrong for God to treat him like this. He even promised that if Job would just shape up, God would reward him: "If you are pure and upright, / surely then [God] will rouse himself for you / and restore to you your rightful place" (Job 8:6).

I don't tend to speak in the accusatory way of Bildad, but when I'm listening to people as a spiritual director I must remind myself not to make the assumptions Bildad made. We can almost never *explain* suffering. Bildad assumed that Job's suffering was because Job had done something wrong. In fact, Job's suffering started because God said that Job was "a blameless and upright man who fears God and turns away from evil" (Job 1:8). Sometimes people do put themselves in the line of suffering. But most of the time suffering is inexplicable.

In group spiritual direction, we want to listen to people from a place of compassion, not judgment. We want to acknowledge both the pain and the mystery of human suffering. And we want to support people as they seek to believe that maybe their suffering will be a means of grace in their lives. "My grace," God said, "is sufficient for you, for power is made perfect in weakness" (2 Corinthians 12:9). But in the midst of deep suffering, it is almost impossible to believe that. In group spiritual direction we dare not shy away from someone's struggle on the faith journey. We sit with them, listen to them, and support them wherever they are in their suffering and pain.

In one of our group spiritual direction sessions Meredith talked about a painful relationship with her sister. While not of Job proportions, the situation was of deep concern to Meredith. She described a serious falling-out with her sibling. She loved her sister but was deeply troubled about the way her sister was treating her. Meredith was hurt and frustrated. She also felt guilty that she was so angry with a family member. Anger, she told herself, was not a feeling she should have. We could hear the pain in her voice as she talked about this relationship. Members of the group asked her questions, inviting her to say more. At one point, someone gently offered the suggestion that Jesus might be sad that this was happening to Meredith. Meredith said afterward that those words, coming after such careful group listening, opened up her heart. She said, "I felt as though the group turned the key of my jail door so I could emerge from the prison of self-recrimination because I was so angry about the way my sister was treating me. The group helped me visualize Jesus comforting me and releasing me from my anger. I began to see that Jesus was not angry with me. He was sad. And he wanted to bring me peace." The freedom and peace that Meredith experienced came through the careful, loving listening the group offered her. This was the kind of listening Job might have liked.

"CHEER UP. I CAN TELL YOU WHAT GOD WANTS."

Job's third friend, Zophar, continues with his friends' attempts to explain and fix Job's problems. He pontificates about the mysteries of God and then says to Job that if he will devote himself to God, he will surely forget his trouble: "Your life will be brighter than the noonday; / its darkness will be like the morning" (Job 11:17). In other words, "Job, I know what God is thinking, and I predict that if you shape up, things will improve."

The temptation to pretend we know God's plan is a strong one. All of us have succumbed to it in one way or another. The point is not whether or not we are *right*; we may be. The point to remember is that it is God's job, not ours, to speak inner truth to our friends. In our companionship of those who are suffering we can say with love, "We don't understand why you are experiencing this difficult situation, but we are here for you. God is faithful. We will support you as you try to believe, even when that seems impossible." Eliphaz, Bildad and Zophar apparently could not offer that kind of comfort.

"Just Listen!"

About this time, Job got fed up with his friends, saying to them, "I would speak to the Almighty, / and I desire to argue my case with God. / As for you, you whitewash with lies; / all of you are worthless physicians. / If you would only keep silent, / that would be your wisdom!" (Job 13:3-5). Later, Job tells them what he really wants: "Listen to me carefully, please listen, / at least do me the favor of listening" (Job 21:1 *The Message*). This was Job's heartfelt plea: Listen to me! Just *listen*. That's all the consolation I want.

I believe that all of us feel this way often. We don't want answers. We may not even want help. We just want someone to listen to us. When Ed, my first spiritual director, listened to me in that old church near the University of Wisconsin, he did not solve my problems. When I left, my friend still had leukemia. Another friend was still getting divorced. My family still faced a possible move across the country. But I was at peace. Ed had listened. Ed had been present to me as God is present to us. Coming along beside. Walking with us. Listening with love. When we share together with a group or with just one person, that is, first of all, what we really want.

Speaking and Listening Well

The author of the book of Ecclesiastes reminds us that there is "a time to keep silence, and a time to speak" (Ecclesiastes 3:7). How do we know the difference? How do we make the choice between the seemingly endless seven days and nights of silence offered by Job's friends, and the apparently endless monologues of advice and accusation that followed? It would be a mistake to think that our listening never includes speaking. We are, after all, companions to one another, encouraging each other to notice God's work within us. I know that I count on spiritual direction conversations to reflect back to me places where I might have blind spots, and to give me fresh perspectives where I have become complacent. Silence is not the only language of spiritual direction. But learning when to speak and when to be silent is not easy. Most of us err on the side of speaking too much. It's an ongoing experience of discernment to know when to talk and when to be quiet. It helps to remember that we are listening in on a conversation someone else is having with God. Most of the time we just listen, perhaps contributing a question or two but still maintaining a quiet presence. Other times the Spirit of God seems to invite us to enter in to the conversation with words.

When the Spirit does prompt us, how do we speak in a way that is loving and life-giving? In group spiritual direction, how can we speak and listen well? How can we, as a group, listen to the one presenting so that he or she can be attentive to the whispers of the Spirit, to the direction of God? I believe there are three things that define the posture of good listeners: a contemplative attitude, an open spirit and a humble perspective. When we listen contemplatively, with openness and with humility, the words that follow our listening will more likely be loving ones. When we listen in this way, we will be able to be with our friends in ways that Job's friends could not.

A contemplative attitude. First of all, good listeners have a contemplative attitude. In religious tradition, contemplating means focusing your awareness on God. But the word *contemplate* refers to more than just being attentive to the Divine. It also means to view (a person or object) with continued attention, to observe thoughtfully, to consider thoroughly and to think deeply. In group spiritual direction we pay attention to God and to each other with a contemplative attitude. Consider what it would look like for members of the group to listen to one another with continued attention, not distracted, not preoccupied, not interrupting. Or to listen with thoughtful and thorough consideration, not judging, not correcting, not busy preparing an answer. Notice how you feel when someone thinks deeply about what you are saying. This kind of contemplative presence describes the kind of listening we do in spiritual direction. The contemplative attitude we offer as we listen is not in a vacuum. It is rooted in God and grows out of our awareness of God's ever-loving presence in all of our lives.

An open spirit. Good listeners have open spirits. In group spiritual direction, those who are listening are "second-in-command" to the one who is presenting. "This kind of listening means that the people receiving attention are allowed to be the experts on their own pain," writes Kenneth Blue. Instead of trying to explain the pain, or whatever it is the person is talking about, we can simply say, "Tell me more about that." This kind of open-ended response affirms the other and validates the other's experience, even if it is very different from our own. Some people have never had anyone listen to them with this kind of openness. To complicate matters more, most people have an inner critic who contradicts them all the time. When we listen with open spirits, we allow our friends to be where they are without judgment and we invite them to experience grace in their present circumstances. "Intense listening is indistinguishable from love, and love heals."

A humble perspective. And finally, good listeners have a humble perspective. Humility in listening means that we let go of preconceived opinions, we let go of the need to be right, we let go of our own insecurities, and we let go of the need to appear wise, good or spiritual. In short, we let go of ourselves in order to be present to the other. This is a high calling and a commitment we will need to return to again and again. Margaret Guenther says that "the greatest gift I could give . . . was not to play social worker or psychotherapist, but to quiet down and wait with her. Be with her. To do this, I had to recognize my discomfort at my own powerlessness."

Indeed, the gift of group spiritual direction is *quieting down and waiting* while another speaks. In that quiet, we can notice that God is with us.

Words for Listening

When we have quieted down, when we have asked God to help us be contemplative, open and humble, then what do we do? What suggestions would we have made to Job's friends if they had asked for advice at the end of the first seven days, before they started talking? What skills or tools can we use that will help us respond lovingly to the one we're listening to? At the risk of over-simplifying, I would like to suggest several ways individuals in a group might respond to the person presenting. These responses, spoken with compassion and love, may give the person presenting encouragement and permission to say more.

Repeat exactly what the person said with an implied question mark at the end, inviting the person to say more. For example, if the person presenting as directee says, "Life is so busy right now, I'm having a hard time noticing God," someone in the group might respond, "It's hard to notice God in your life right now?"

Ask for more information about the person's experience. If the directee says, "I just feel so discouraged about my work situation," someone could respond, "Could you say a little more about that?"

Say what the person said, using different words, again with an implied question mark. For instance, if the presenter says, "It just seemed like too much for God to ask me to do," a possible response might be, "You felt overwhelmed?"

Describe what you're hearing, and then ask if that's correct. For example, someone might begin by saying, "When I go to church, I worry about saying the right thing, knowing what to do, how to behave." In response, someone else might say, "It sounds like you're worried about what people will think of you. Is that correct?"

Don't say anything. A directee could say, "I think I may be ready to deal with my father's alcoholism." Nod your head. Maintain eye contact. Wait.

Offer some connections from several parts of the conversation. The person presenting might talk about several things going on in life. "On Saturday I had a really hard day with my daughter . . . Last week my boss said they might have to downsize the company . . . I didn't get asked to be on the membership committee this year. . . ." Someone could respond, "It sounds like you've been experiencing some disappointments in some important relationships in your life."

If appropriate, ask if the person is sensing any direction from God. At some point in the sharing, the directee might say, "This all just seems so confusing to me. One minute I think I should take the job and move out of town, and the next minute I think I'd rather not bother." Someone in the group could ask, "In your quieter reflections, what nudges from God do you sense as you consider your options?"

These are just a few ways of listening and responding that help the person go deeper into their experience. One or two responses like this may help draw out of the person truth that is already there. Jesus promised that the Spirit would guide us "into all the truth" (John 16:13). Our job as listeners is to help our friend listen to the Spirit. Anything we can say or not say that will help clarify their own experiences and observations takes them closer to the Truth in their inner being.

JUST LISTEN

Recently I was the one in need of this kind of loving listening. Between the two of us, my husband and I lost three parents, all of whom died within three weeks of each other. Our friends surrounded us with love, food and sympathy. But when I went to my lectio-spiritual direction group, I was full to overflowing with things I needed to talk about. I needed to describe how each death had happened. I needed to say where I was, how I felt, who I talked to, what I did. Then I needed to talk about how I changed through the event. And how I hadn't changed. I needed to say how I was feeling at the present moment. There was nothing any of my listening friends could do to change the circumstances. I certainly did not want them to try to change me! I wanted them to *just listen*. And they did. My friends loved me by listening. They listened as I described the details of my past weeks. They encouraged me to share by asking questions that showed me they were interested. They affirmed my many conflicting emotions. They asked questions until they sensed a shift in me from anxious discomfort to a more hopeful settledness. They loved me right where I was. Their love helped me experience God's love even in the difficult, unexpected experience.

In group spiritual direction, as we listen well, we provide regular opportunities to extend comfort, support and perspective to those we love. As we listen to one another, we come together as fellow travelers, noticing the landscape, sharing our maps and encouraging each other on the journey.

5

ASKING LIFE-GIVING QUESTIONS

Henri Nouwen, a well-known teacher and author, taught that questions are at the heart of spiritual direction. Nouwen acknowledged that questions like "Who am I?" "How does God speak to me?" and "Where do I belong?" do not have easy answers. But what is most needed, he says, is to affirm the validity of the questions: "What needs to be said is: 'Yes, yes indeed, these are the questions. Don't hesitate to raise them. Don't be afraid to enter them. Don't turn away from living them. Don't worry if you don't have a final answer on the tip of your tongue.'"

In group spiritual direction the goal is not to answer life's questions. The goal is to draw closer to God in the midst of the questions. Many times it is in embracing our questions that we move more deeply into God's love. In spiritual direction we are saying to one another:

You seek answers to what cannot be fully known. I don't know either, but I will help you search. I offer no solutions, no final answers. I am as weak and limited as you are. But we are not alone. Where there is charity and love, God is there. Together, we form community. Together we continue the spiritual search.

In group spiritual direction, we continue the search, not by solving problems or answering the questions, but by validating the questions. Often we do this by asking more questions. We ask about the directee's experiences. We ask about the directee's perspectives. We ask about the directee's questions. One of the greatest gifts we can give another is to ask a meaningful question. With our questions, we are inviting further exploration into whatever the directee is presenting. "In the ministry of spiritual direction, there are no right answers, only clearer visions of ever deeper questions," Margaret Guenther writes.

Jesus' ministry was full of questions. He did not need to know the answers to his questions. After all, he was God. So his questions must have been for the sake of those who came to him for help or healing. Before Jesus healed the blind man Bartimaeus, he asked him, "What do you want me to do for you?" (see Mark 10:49-52). It seems to me that would have been quite obvious. But Jesus asked anyway. Perhaps Bartimaeus needed to verbalize what he most wanted. "Rabbi," he said, "I want to see" (v. 51 NIV).

The question Jesus asked Bartimaeus is a good one for spiritual direction. "What is it you would like Jesus to do for you?" Exploring that question in the presence of loving friends may help the directee access a new dimension of God's love.

Jesus also asked a rather strange question when a woman came to him with a very private illness. She had had her period ("a flow of blood") for twelve years. Not willing to speak up, she just touched Jesus' robe (see Mark 5:25-34). Jesus asked, "Who touched my clothes?" Even his disciples thought that was a strange thing to ask. They said, "You see the crowd pressing in on you; how can you say, 'Who touched me?'" Jesus probably knew who touched him. But by asking the question, he drew attention to her and allowed all the people around her to know that she was healed. This was especially important in her society because the woman was considered "unclean" and was isolated from her friends and community (see Leviticus 15:25). Jesus' question led to a personal encounter, and the woman was not only healed but also restored to her friends and neighbors.

NOT A POPULAR CALLING

Asking loving questions is a countercultural phenomenon. We live in a culture where having answers is more popular than asking questions. Furthermore, in this media-saturated age we have answers to questions we didn't even know we were asking. In the midst of the onslaught of information around us, the art of asking questions is losing ground. In normal conversation we often forget about questions altogether. We're eager to impart information, opinions and suggestions, but we forget about having inquiring minds. But asking questions moves us out of our attempts to have all the answers or to have a better story than the last one told. We show love to someone else by being willing to move away from center stage in a conversation and ask a question. The person asking the question allows their friend to be the authority, to tell a story or to just talk about something personally meaningful. Learning to ask good questions—while not easy—changes us and helps us focus on others.

Even more, good questions give life to the process of group spiritual direction. Sometimes asking questions leads to the healing of deeper needs than are first presented, as Jesus did when he healed the woman with the flow of blood. This was the case for Julie, a young professional woman who came regularly to group spiritual direction in our church. She stayed a bit aloof from the group but her regular attendance indicated that the experience was meaningful. The night she was presenting she started out by saying that she hadn't come to church for several Sundays. "It's just too hard to get up in time to come," she said. Several of us in the group asked her questions to help her talk more about what she was experiencing. At first our questions were rather general: "Is the new church schedule a problem?" "Do you like the new service?" "Is something missing for you at church?" As she explored her thoughts and feelings, her eyes teared up. "Coming to church has been too hard for me," she said, "ever since my divorce became final." At that point, the conversation opened up and she was able to talk about the very personal and private experience of the death of her marriage, and the subsequent experiences of loneliness and self-doubt. We continued to ask questions, but now they were more personal, inviting her to talk about whatever she wanted to share concerning her divorce and the impact it had on her life and her relationship with God. In another setting, the questions we asked might have seemed too personal. But because our group had developed a safe, caring community, we were able to ask loving questions that helped Julie experience healing love in the midst of the pain.

Questions are the backbone of the group spiritual direction process. A question like "Can you give me an example of that?" invites the directee to talk more. "What was that like for you?" invites him to share his own experience more fully. "How do you feel about that situation?" is an invitation for a directee to explore both her positive and her negative feelings.

Many people want to ask good questions but don't know how. Other people are not used to the kinds of questions that are lifegiving in a spiritual direction encounter. The following lists are examples of questions that might be helpful in group spiritual direction. These are just suggestions. Hopefully they will trigger for you a few questions of your own that you can ask to help your friend hear the Spirit's gentle direction in life.

QUESTIONS TO GET STARTED

When people arrive for group spiritual direction, they may know exactly what they want to talk about. Perhaps they have a troubling relationship, or a situation they'd like to talk about, or maybe they just want to celebrate a milestone on their spiritual journey. If someone comes with an agenda, that's the place to start.

Often, however, people come not having anything in mind for the spiritual direction time. After the time of getting settled and quieting down, when the facilitator asks the person presenting to begin, they might say, "Well, I don't really have anything specific to talk about today. . . ." This may be followed by an uncomfortable pause when everyone is wondering where to go from here. Here are a few questions that can help get the person started:

- What was life like for you today?

- Can you describe the time today when you felt the most free? When did you feel least free?

- What is something you desire in your life these days? Can you talk a bit about your desires for yourself?

These questions are not ends in themselves. As the directee answers a rather general question about life, something may come into focus that calls for more questions and further discussion. For example, asking about moments when the person felt free on that particular day may lead to a discussion about what parts of life seem the most Spirit-filled for the directee. This would reflect the teaching in Scripture that "where the Spirit of the Lord is, there is freedom" (2 Corinthians 3:17). Or asking about the directee's desires may lead to a discussion about the teaching that God "will give you the desires of your heart" (Psalm 37:4). You might continue the discussion by asking the directee where he or she senses that desire came from. Is it from God? Is it rooted in any other desires that are from God? By starting with a simple question, we can sometimes help the directee interact with the Spirit of God in light of specific, daily experiences.

NOTICING GOD IN DAILY LIFE

Most people who come for group spiritual direction want to grow closer to God. It's tempting to think that drawing closer to God is an out-of-the-ordinary experience apart from daily life. But Jesus taught that this is not so. Jesus spoke of "the kingdom of God." This kingdom (the place where God reigns) is not somewhere else, outside of us. Rather, Jesus said "the kingdom of God is within you" (Luke 17:21 NIV). Since we cannot actually *see* the kingdom of God, Jesus used word pictures to describe it. And the words Jesus used were amazingly practical. Jesus compared the kingdom of God to everyday events of the time, like a farmer planting seeds (Matthew 13:3-9), a woman putting yeast in bread (Matthew 13:33), someone looking for a lost coin (Luke 15:8-10), a parent with a rebellious child (Luke 15:11-32). As we experience these very ordinary events, we experience them within the context of the kingdom of God.

This is why spiritual direction questions often focus on our inner responses to our daily lives. How we respond to the events of our everyday lives *is* our spiritual journey. In groups and with individuals, questions allow the directee to notice the experience of God's grace and love in very practical, everyday ways. The following questions are ones that can specifically help the directee do just that. (Don't ask all of them! These are just questions in my own "mental file" that might help the conversation get started.)

- In the last twenty-four hours, what gave you joy? Sorrow?
- Who in your life (past or present) has given you a taste of God's love?
- What activities in your life seem to draw you to God? What

activities in your life seem to pull you away from God?

- When or where are you most likely to be aware of God's presence? When or where are you least aware of God's presence?

- In the last day or two, when or where were you most aware of the presence of God in your life?

These questions are all intended to help the directee *notice* God. Behind every question is an open invitation to talk about practical and daily experiences of the presence of God.

QUESTIONS ABOUT THE SPIRITUAL JOURNEY

Group spiritual direction, then, is about daily life. More specifically, it's about our everyday spiritual journeys. It's about how we relate to God. It's about how we communicate or do not communicate with Love. Being with a group of people where we are free to talk honestly and personally about our relationship with God is certainly a unique and grace-filled experience, which means that, as we participate in group spiritual direction, we need to be able to ask questions specifically about the spiritual life. Here are a few suggestions:

- How would you describe your relationship with God today?

- What is prayer like for you? What kind of prayer is most appealing to you?

- When do you remember first thinking about God?

- How do you experience temptation in your life?

- What do you do really well? What do you think you are gifted to do?

- What is your soul longing for today?

- How is it for you when you read Scripture?

- When are you bored with your spiritual journey?

Again, I never ask all of these questions at once. I just keep in mind a variety of questions that I can draw from that may help give signposts on the spiritual journey.

QUESTIONS TO GO DEEPER

After the group has launched into the heart of the spiritual direction session, it may be helpful to ask a few questions to invite the person presenting to look with deeper clarity at how God is intersecting the event or relationship being discussed. Here are a few questions that might facilitate going deeper.

- How is your view of God changing because of this experience?

- What person in your own life acts (or acted) the way you perceive God to be acting in your life right now?

- How would you like God to help you in this?

- What do you think the Spirit of Jesus might be whispering to your spirit in this situation? (See 1 Kings 19:11-13 for an example of someone hearing God whisper.)

- How are you being changed by this relationship or set of circumstances?

- How would you most like God to touch your soul, your inner being, at this time in your life?

Sometimes even a good question is a dead-end street. The group may reach a bit of a standstill, unsure of where to go. When this happens, it may help to ask the directee a very broad question:

- It is there any question you would like us to ask you?

- How do you sense we could be helpful to you now?

Asking either of these questions can be a loving way to return to whatever the directee really wants to talk about.

Questions for Closing

The purpose of group spiritual direction is not to solve problems. It is to provide an environment where we can help one another embrace the presence of God in the context of the particular piece of life being presented. As the time of group spiritual direction draws to a close, it is helpful to ask a question or two to help the person describe his or her sense of the direction of God. Here are some possible questions you can use to do this:

- How would you like to experience God in the next few weeks?

- Do you sense any invitation from God in this?

- What would you *like* God's invitation to be?

- How do you hope your relationship with God will change as a result of this time together?

- What do you see as the first step on this next phase of your spiritual journey?

Again, probably one of these questions will be enough. Whatever the question, it should lead to a sense of closure for the person presenting as well as provide a sense that the journey will continue.

Questions Not to Ask

As wonderful as questions can be, some questions are simply not helpful. They can be manipulative or superficial. Sometimes they're so loaded with the suggested answer that they fall on deaf ears. A really good question is open-ended. It allows the other person to respond in any way she'd like. It allows for exploration. It gives permission for the other person to talk deeply if he chooses. It is invitational and welcoming.

Often (but not always) questions that start with *why* or that can be answered with a yes or no are unhelpful. "Why do you think you're in this situation?" "Did you ask God about this?" or "Do you think

God is taking care of you?" are all examples of questions that probably won't lead to deeper discussion or revelation.

Sometimes questions lose their value because we ask too many. Thoughtful questions invite thoughtful replies that may take time to form. Another question asked too soon may interrupt the process. This is a particular risk in group spiritual direction where several people are acting as the director and each one of them may have a question. Go slowly. Allow for silence in between questions. Be sensitive to the Spirit. My friend Miriam pointed out that sometimes when we speak up too soon, even with a good question, we are actually interrupting the dialogue the directee is having with God. Miriam, a midwife who is now in training to be a spiritual director, told me that this kind of listening is amazing and difficult for her. She said that she's just learning that not everyone processes things the same extroverted way she does. She has learned to allow for longer spaces of silence and to notice when people need conversation and when people need quiet. "What amazes me most," she says, "is that before, I didn't know I was interrupting [their dialogue with God]. At least I was interrupting with some people. Like women in labor, they all need different styles. Because I process differently, it is harder for me to learn to be with people who process at a different rate."

Spiritual direction is an art, not a science. It is a charism, a gift from God, not just a skill to be learned. Sometimes people in the group do need to speak up, perhaps even make a suggestion or two. But we need to always remember the old adage, "Only speak when it improves upon silence." The words of Ecclesiastes come back to us: There is a time to speak and a time to be silent. Questions often help us when we are not sure which time it is.

6

EXPLORING THOUGHTS
AND FEELINGS

 ⌘

A year or two after we began offering group spiritual direction in our church, a friend asked me if he could visit the first session of the fall term to see what spiritual direction is like. He wasn't sure he wanted to sign on, but he was intrigued. During the evening, I found myself watching him out of the corner of my eye. He looked uncomfortable. Afterward he said to me, "I didn't know it would be so much about feelings."

His response didn't surprise me. Newcomers to spiritual direction often notice that there is a lot of talk about *feelings*. Many people take offense at this. While few come right out and ask, they seem to want to know, "Do I have to leave my brain at the door when I come for spiritual direction?" Let me assure you that this is most definitely not true! Our minds, our brains, are certainly an important way God reaches our souls.

But even as I offer this assurance, I know that spiritual directors often talk about "moving from the head down to the heart." It's easy to hear this as a dismissal of the brain (the head) and bias for the heart, which is often assumed to be feelings. This, however, is an unfortunate misunderstanding, so before we go further into a description of group spiritual direction, I would like to look at the roots of this misunderstanding, the connection between our experiences of thinking and feeling, and why spiritual direction—both individual and group—sometimes emphasizes feelings.

Do I Think or Do I Feel?

The dichotomy between thoughts and feelings is misleading. It's like trying to describe the difference between presenting truth in a scientific report or in a poem. Jesus taught in ways that respected both thinking and feeling. He informed the mind with his didactic teaching and theological observations. But, through stories and parables, Jesus also invited his listeners to experience the feelings of the truths he was describing.

To emphasize either thoughts or feelings at the expense of the other is to look at human experience as *flat* rather than multidimensional. Consider, for example, what it would be like to sit in a concert hall and listen to a performance of Beethoven's *Ninth Symphony*. As the music swells to its triumph, some people in the audience hear the musical transitions and know when the violins carry the melody and when the woodwinds take over. Others in the audience do not perceive the changes in the movements of the music, but they love the symphony because it stirs their emotions and their feelings. Those who think about the music and those who feel the music both walk away with a sense of awe. Perhaps unaware of the roots of this awe, they know that their hearts have been moved.

The Place of the Heart

Moving from the concert hall back to spiritual direction, consider what happens in our hearts as we move forward on our spiritual journeys. In the Bible, the word *heart* actually means "the intellect, memory, emotions, desires and will." To talk about "moving from the head down to the heart" does not mean to move from thinking to feeling. It means to move from theoretical knowledge to actual experience. It means to move from believing a truth to living a truth. To speak from the heart, in the truest biblical sense, is to speak from the depths of our being, including both our thoughts and our feelings.

The heart (including our thoughts and our feelings) is where the Spirit of God lives within us. The apostle Paul wrote that "God has sent the Spirit of his Son into our hearts, crying, 'Abba! Father!'" (Galatians 4:6). *Abba* means "papa." Spiritual direction, then, is about the intimate relationship between a child and a loving parent. This relationship starts and ends with our hearts—our perceptions, our experiences, our feelings and our wills. We cannot separate our thoughts and our feelings from the experiences of our souls. With our thoughts and our feelings, we say, "Abba, Father, you are my God."

A SOURCE OF INFORMATION

Why, then, as my friend observed, does spiritual direction seem to emphasize feelings? One of the reasons is because feelings are a source of information about how we view God, ourselves and others. Years ago someone gave me this definition: *Feelings are the spontaneous response we give to our interpretation of an event.* Our feelings will reflect whatever interpretation we have. This is true even if we're unaware of our interpretations and even if our interpretations are inaccurate. In this way, our feelings give us information about what we *really* think about events and relationships. When we pay attention to our feelings we may notice unconscious interpretations. Then we can ask ourselves, is this feeling a response to truth or to falsehood?

Look at how this might play out on our spiritual journey. Our feelings may show us what we really believe about God, even if we think we believe something different. For instance, I grew up in a family with very high standards, which I never met. When I became a Christian, I learned that God loved me. But I also assumed that God's expectations for me were as unattainable as my parents' expectations for me had been. This was an inaccurate and unbiblical understanding of God, but one which I never questioned. By the time I became an adult, I had a voice inside of me shouting out that my mistakes, my failures and my inadequacies made God mad. I interpreted many of the events in my life in light of the assumption that I was not good enough and that God was disappointed in me. Needless to say, the feelings I had in response to that interpretation were not joy and peace. Instead, I felt ashamed, sad, guilty and inadequate. These feelings contradicted what I said I believed about God's unconditional love, so for years I refused to acknowledge that I felt this way. But the weight of these negative feelings eventually led me to turn to God and seek truth and love. When I really listened to what my negative feelings were saying, I could see that they were my own spontaneous responses to an inaccurate view of God.

This is something that still comes up frequently when I talk with my spiritual director. The voice of the inner critic is so loud that often I cannot hear the whispers of the Spirit. I say I believe that God is full of grace and that God loves me, but my feelings of guilt and fear tell me that I don't really believe that. Sometimes just describing my feelings helps loosen their grip on me. In addition, my spiritual director helps me reinterpret my journey in ways that are more in keeping with what I believe about God's love for me. And sometimes in moments of silence, in the presence of my spiritual director, God touches my heart and heals a wounded spot.

Growing awareness of our interpretations about God and ourselves is also a benefit of group spiritual direction. In one group session, Allison was the directee. She presented her struggle with chronic discouragement. She said that she never felt as though she performed well enough at work and struggled with the fear that she didn't have the skills she needed to do a good job. Even though Allison hadn't received negative feedback, she couldn't shake her discouragement. As the group listened and responded to her concerns, Allison blurted out, "I just feel so inadequate!" Responding to this, someone in the group asked her when before in her life she had felt inadequate. She replied, "All the time!" Members of the group invited her to say more by asking questions: How did she experience this feeling of inadequacy "all the time"? What was her sense about whether or not her feeling of inadequacy was rooted in reality, fear or something else? How would she like to respond to this feeling in light of God's presence in her life? As Allison processed her experiences in the welcoming atmosphere of the group, she began to believe that what she thought was a personal defect could become an invitation to embrace God's grace, strength and love in her life. When she left the group session, she knew she would still have to deal with feelings of discouragement, but she had renewed hope that her friends and the Holy Spirit would be companioning with her.

The Treasures of the Heart

The "treasures of our hearts" are the places in our lives where we invest the most emotional, intellectual and spiritual energy. When something consumes our attention, it's probably something our heart treasures, whether we know it or not. Jesus said, "Where your treasure is, there your heart will be also" (Matthew 6:21). Since spiritual direction is about the journey of our hearts toward God, looking for what we treasure becomes an important part of the conversation.

Spiritual direction is a safe place where we can look at any consuming area of life and listen to God's perspective about whatever it is we treasure. For instance, I'm not usually aware that I "treasure" being available to meet the needs of others. But I often find myself in relationships which consume a lot of my energy and attention. When

I meet with my friends in group spiritual direction, I sometimes complain about the stress I feel in these relationships. I may share my feelings of frustration, and of being overwhelmed and underappreciated. I often start with these negative feelings. By asking me ever-deeper questions about what is really going on inside of me, my friends accompany me to the realization that my feelings are rooted in my desire to fix other people's problems. In the quiet loving experience of spiritual direction, I hear God whispering, *Alice, that's my job.* On a cognitive level I know that. But in my "heart" I treasure my own ability to fix or control life, mine and others. Through the process of spiritual direction, I am able to let go of that treasure, at least a little bit. When I let go, I often find that God gives me an experience of grace and peace, something I treasure even more.

Our Neglected Feelings

Another reason spiritual direction emphasizes feelings is that in our Western culture, the thinking side of our hearts often gets more attention than the feeling side. We affirm our thinking with teaching and creeds and books that nourish our minds and then often subject our feelings to logical thinking, with thoughts like, *I shouldn't feel this way because I know God loves me.* Our thinking minds try to tell us how to feel. If we do this frequently, we may ignore our feelings altogether. But stressful feelings are like the "fix engine" light on a dashboard, telling us that something is wrong inside. Feelings are a gift from God reminding us to notice places where truth has not penetrated our inner being. This is why spiritual direction extends a strong invitation to pay attention to feelings, to embrace the truth in our feelings which our mind may be resisting.

I had been meeting with a young woman for some time. One day she was telling me about a very difficult relationship. Tears were running down her face. I commented that her situation would make me sad too. She responded, "Oh, do you think I'm sad? How did you know that?" She had ignored her feelings for so long that even her tears couldn't tell her how she felt. Feelings aren't more important than thinking, but often they give us unfiltered feedback about what we really believe about God, ourselves and our faith. Because of cultural influences, temperamental preferences or even theological misunderstandings we may ignore our feelings. When we do this, we miss a significant avenue God may use to heal us and help us.

HIDING IN THE BUSHES

Another reason why spiritual direction encourages talk about feelings is that many of us have taught ourselves to hide our feelings. Like Adam and Eve, we hide when God comes looking for us (Genesis 3:8-10). Hurt, anger, jealousy and fear are all feelings we probably do not want God or anyone else to see in us. I tried to hide my negative feelings from my husband when we were first married because I was convinced that if he knew about them, he wouldn't love me. Many of us spend enormous amounts of energy hiding our feelings—especially the negative ones—from others, from God and even from ourselves. But when we stuff our negative feelings into the dark corners of our soul, those very feelings control us. When we bring them to light and allow ourselves to feel them, they no longer have control over us. Spiritual direction can help us reach this place of freedom.

We may try to hide positive feelings as well as negative feelings, however. If, for instance, we feel like jumping for joy that we did something well, we may restrain ourselves because we fear others will think we're bragging. Spiritual direction helps us here too. Susan, a member of a group I was in a few years ago, struggled with the mysterious feeling she had when she discovered that people in her church saw her as mature and wise. As we asked her to tell us more about her experience and continued to ask her questions, she discovered that what she was feeling was joy—the special joy that comes from using the gifts God has given us. Susan's response to identifying this positive feeling was not pride but gratitude.

Sometimes I try to hide my feelings about my own spiritual journey. I may shy away from telling a friend about a particularly meaningful devotional time because I'm afraid I will be misunderstood. I'm afraid my quiet musings will not be taken seriously. I don't want to hide, but I'm learning that I do. This is one of the things I love about my spiritual direction group. My friends are helping me come out of the bushes of fear by welcoming and affirming my walk with God.

We are inclined to hide from others and from ourselves. Spiritual direction provides the safe place we need to express not only our thoughts but also our deep feelings. Naming and experiencing our feelings in a quiet, safe place opens up space for God to touch our souls.

Extending a Welcome for Feelings

In group spiritual direction, we extend to others the grace to express feelings without pressuring them to talk more than they're able. Once again questions are our most helpful tool. Questions like the following ones might assist in bringing feelings into the light, where healing occurs.

- Can you say more about the _____ [anger, fear, perplexity, etc.]?

- How does your body respond to that feeling?

- When in this relationship or situation are you most likely to have that feeling?

- As you think about the issue you're processing, what feelings rise up within you?

- When in your life before have you had the feeling you're describing now?

- Would you say you're feeling glad, mad, sad, confused or angry about this situation or relationship?

- What adjective describes how you feel about the person or event you're talking about?

- Would you like us just to sit with you for a few minutes in silence to let you feel that feeling?

One or two of these questions may invite the person presenting to spend time noticing and listening to his or her feelings. We can also simply notice their feelings by making observations such as, "I hear anger [or frustration or hurt] in your voice. Is that what you're feeling?" I remember one time when I was feeling joy and peace, my spiritual director said to me, "I see that in your face." Our feedback may validate what the person is feeling.

UNHELPFUL RESPONSES

Just as there are questions and responses that are helpful, so there are things we might say that are distinctly not helpful. One of the most common unhelpful responses is "I know just how you feel." While it might be useful to briefly mention how we might have felt ("That would have made me mad.") it is not helpful to assume that we know how someone else would actually feel. It's also not helpful to try to generate optimism. No one wants to hear, "Don't worry— it will get better." Or, "Trust God. God always knows best." Or, "At least you don't have cancer like so and so." Sometimes all we can do is ask, "What would be helpful to you right now?" We need special grace to companion people experiencing difficult feelings, to help them turn to God without pushing them or trivializing what they really feel.

PEACE BEYOND UNDERSTANDING

The goal in focusing on feelings is not to wallow in them. Nor is it just to clarify thinking. The goal is to notice and embrace the presence of God in this experience. When this happens, the peace that comes "transcends all understanding" (Philippians 4:7 NIV). In other words, we cannot *think* our way into God's peace; it's beyond understanding. The Bible also says that the love of God "surpasses knowledge" (Ephesians 3:19). No matter how much we *know*, God's love is deeper, so sometimes the route to this peace-beyond-knowing is through our feelings. Spiritual direction provides a unique place where feelings are welcome and helps us experience God in ways that are beyond understanding and knowledge.

7

MEDITATING ON

SCRIPTURE TOGETHER

✍

Mrs. Duncan was my third-grade Sunday school teacher. She was also the first person I had ever met who took the Bible seriously. Really seriously. Her agenda for those of us in her class was that we memorize Bible verses. Lots of Bible verses. Fortunately for me, she rewarded our efforts with prizes, including glow-in-the-dark figures of little girls praying, little boys praying and Jesus himself praying. I didn't like memorizing the verses, but I did like the figurines. My efforts soon resulted in a nice collection.

By the time I graduated from high school and entered college, I had moved on from glow-in-the-dark figurines. And I too, like Mrs. Duncan, took the Bible seriously. One of the first activities I committed to in college was a weekly Bible study. I don't remember what we studied, but I do know that we always looked first at the facts in the passage, then we tried hard to interpret the facts, and finally, we applied all of that information to our lives. Those Bible studies were rich experiences, and I am very, very grateful for them.

SOMETHING DIFFERENT

Since then, I have discovered that there are other ways of reading and experiencing Scripture. In college I read Scripture to gather all the information I could about God, Jesus and the life of faith. This worked well for me then, as I was a young believer and needed all the information I could get. But as my journey continued, I've found that increasing my bank of information is not the same as deepening my relationship with God.

Robert Mulholland, in his book *Shaped by the Word,* says that we often read the Bible as informational readers. Informational reading is linear and analytical: "We seek to master the text. We seek to grasp it, to get our minds around it, to bring it under *our* control." In *formational* reading, on the other hand, the point is to "allow the text to master you." Mulholland's observations resonate with my own experience of reading the Bible through the years. I knew a great deal from opportunities like my third-grade Bible memorization program and my college Bible studies. But I longed for more. I longed to draw closer to God, to be transformed by grace. In this longing, I found an invitation from God to experience Scripture in a new way.

The two ways I learned to read the Bible were new to me but, like spiritual direction, they are ancient in their tradition. We will look together at these two formational ways of reading the Bible and then consider how they might be incorporated into the spiritual direction experience. Formational reading of Scripture fits well with spiritual direction because in both disciplines the goal is to nurture ever-deepening communion with God.

LECTIO DIVINA

One of these ancient ways of reading is called lectio divina, which means "spiritual reading" in Latin. Lectio divina is a way of reading the Bible very, very slowly. Usually only a few verses are read at a time. Sometimes only one verse is read. There are generally six parts to the lectio divina experience.

1. Start with a minute or two of silence. Breathe deeply and acknowledge your willingness to let go of your own agenda and listen to the Spirit of God speaking through the Word.

2. Read the verses. Read the verses again. Read the verses out loud. Be still and quiet again.

3. Think about what the verses say. Try to hear the passage as though you're hearing it for the first time. Notice what word, phrase or idea stands out to you. Stay with that word or idea in your mind, thinking about what it means.

4. Dialogue with God about the word, phrase or idea. Tell God how you respond to it—what feelings you have about it. Pour out your heart to God as you talk about how this word or idea might apply to something in your life right now.

5. Wait quietly again before God. Listen to whatever God is saying to you around this word, phrase or idea. Notice if God seems to be inviting you to embrace a truth or experience a change.

6. Conclude your time by noticing if there is anything you need to do in order to respond to the Word in your daily life.

It should be clear from this description that the goal of lectio is not to gain larger quantities of information but to deeply experience the truth of a small amount of Scripture. Michael Casey, a Cistercian monk, says:

this is good

> Repetition is the soul of genuine lectio. It is a right brain activity; we do not grasp the entire content immediately but in a circular manner. We read and advance, then we go back and read again. . . . The more we can slow down our reading, the more

likely it is that we will catch sight of something unexpected.
. . . The point about lectio divina is that it not only enlightens
the mind, it also massages the will.

He also says that "lectio divina is an element in a lifelong process
of turning toward God." Reading the Bible in this way requires an
openness to God and a willingness to listen to God's Spirit speaking God's Word into our daily lives. This is why lectio divina fits so
well with spiritual direction, where we seek to nurture a disposition
ready to experience God's love and grace in all aspects of life.

In responding to God's Word deep within the inner resources
of our hearts, we are following in the tradition of Moses, of the Old
Testament. He said to the Israelites: "The word is very near you; it is
in your mouth and in your heart so you may obey it" (Deuteronomy
30:14 NIV). It's good for us to remember that when Moses said that,
almost no one had access to written Scriptures. Informational reading was not an option for the Israelites! Rather, the word of God
was *inside* them. Lectio divina is one way to get Scripture inside our
hearts, even today.

USING THE IMAGINATION

Another ancient way of reading Scripture is to actually enter into the
Bible passage with the imagination. Ignatius of Loyola, a fifteenth-
century convert to Christianity, is credited with introducing this
way of reading. While recovering from a war wound he began reading the Bible. Author Margaret Silf writes that for Ignatius this way
of reading became a way of praying.

He began to find himself, in imagination, present in the scenes,
conversations, and stories of the Gospels, and he began to participate in the plots of these stories. It was the start, for him,
of an adventure into imaginative prayer that was to become a
most powerful catalyst for the growth of his personal relation-

ship with God, a method of prayer that is just as vividly available to us today.

Ignatius went on to develop the well-known "Spiritual Exercises of Saint Ignatius," which make generous use of the imagination.

When we read Scripture using our imagination, we picture ourselves in the setting of the Scripture passage. We ask ourselves what it would have been like to actually be in that time and place. We notice what catches our attention in the scene before us. We notice what we see, what we hear, even what we smell. We notice how we feel, what questions we might ask and how we might respond to whatever is happening in this event. This works particularly well with the Gospel narratives but can be used in most parts of the Bible.

The roots of imaginative reading of Scripture go far back into Christian history. We know St. Augustine used it, for example, to embrace the personal truth in the story of Jesus calming the storm in Mark 4:35-41. The passage gives the account of Jesus, asleep in a boat, until his frantic friends woke him and urged him to do something about the fierce storm surrounding them. Jesus "got up, rebuked the wind and said to the waves, 'Quiet! Be still!' Then the wind died down and it was completely calm" (Mark 4:39 NIV). In writing about this, Augustine went far beyond the historical facts of the event. He said:

> When you have to listen to abuse, that means you are being buffeted by the wind. When your anger is roused, you are being tossed by the waves. . . . On hearing yourself insulted, you long to retaliate; but the joy of revenge brings with it another kind of misfortune—shipwreck. Why is this? Because Christ is asleep in you. What do I mean? I mean you have forgotten his presence. Rouse him, then; remember him, let him keep watch within you, pay heed to him.

Augustine calls upon his readers to do much more than observe the facts. He asks them to enter into the experience of shipwreck, not just in its historical format, but in an everyday way. When we experience insults and anger, he says, we are to rouse the Christ within us—a powerful image that we can only grasp with our imaginations.

Augustine lived from A.D. 354 to 430. His observations about Jesus rebuking the storm are relevant today because with the imagination we can traverse time. But his observations, growing out of his own imaginative interpretation, are not the only way to enter into this story. I have heard from many people who've read this passage imaginatively and come up with different meanings. For some, it is enough just to know that God is in their boat. Others have identified elements of the storm with circumstances in their lives which need to change. Still others are blessed by Jesus' ability to calm storms, whether they are within us or outside of us. The imagination is a human tool the Spirit has used to teach people throughout the ages.

Some people, however, find the idea of using our imagination in this way to be a little troubling, since Scripture is inspired. They fear that using human imagination may lead to misunderstanding and untruth. But the power of the Spirit of God can permeate and use every human faculty we have. Jesus himself employed the imagination in the stories he told. In his parables he engaged his listeners through their imaginations, in order to teach them truths about God. When we use our imagination to understand Scripture, we're simply placing ourselves into the scenes and teachings of the Bible and noticing our responses to God. Furthermore, in many ways our own lives are parables. Reading the Bible imaginatively helps us be more attuned to God's love and grace in the parables of our lives and our world.

Reading Scripture with the lectio divina format and with my imagination has transformed my life. As helpful as my college Bible studies were, I didn't really capture the magnificence of God's Word, alive today. The Bible, like Jesus, is God's expression of divine love. Jesus was the Word of God made flesh. The Bible is the Word of God in language. The author of Hebrews wrote that "the word of God is living and active" (Hebrews 4:12). This means that God's Word, in Jesus and in Scripture, is not dead but alive.

EXPERIENCING SCRIPTURE IN SPIRITUAL DIRECTION

As I have experimented with reading Scripture for transformation rather than just for information, I've been able to see God's love enfleshed in my own life and in the lives of those around me. The Word of God in Jesus and the Word of God in Scripture are alive, and they enable me to see the Word of God everywhere. Experiencing Scripture in this way dovetails with my experiences of God in spiritual direction. Both disciplines help me notice God and be attentive to the Spirit's continuing revelation. Formational reading of Scripture and spiritual direction go hand in hand on my own spiritual journey. *NOTICING... attention*

Let me give a few examples of how Scripture can be used in transformational ways in individual spiritual direction. Then we'll look at this experience in group spiritual direction.

Lectio divina. I often use lectio divina when I am meeting with someone for individual spiritual direction. As I listen to the directee, it's as though I'm listening to two people at once—to the directee and to the Holy Spirit. Sometimes I sense the Spirit bringing a passage of Scripture to my mind. If that sense persists, I might ask the person if they would like to look at a short passage together. We begin this lectio divina experience with a minute or two of silence. Then I read the passage slowly, usually two or three times. I ask the directee to sit as long as they'd like and reflect on what part of the passage stood out. Whenever my friend is ready, we talk about that significant part, how it might apply to everyday life, and whether or not there seems to be an invitation to them from God in the passage. Almost always something significant comes out of the reading and our discussion. If not, we let it go. I never push too hard in this experience.

One of the interesting things to me as the spiritual director is that the person I'm meeting with rarely focuses on the part of the Bible passage that I thought was most significant. This is reassuring to me because it reminds me that the Spirit is at work in both of our lives, perhaps reminding me of a text for entirely different reasons than what the directee will experience. In this, as in every part of spiritual direction, I need to trust the Spirit's guidance in both my heart and the directee's heart. It is never the place of the director to push a certain agenda. Often it's quite surprising, to say the least, to see what comes out of these experiences of lectio divina.

Imaginative reading. Imaginative reading of Scripture is also often part of individual spiritual direction. For example, I was meeting with someone who had been struggling with the same problem in her life for years. Nothing seemed to help. As we talked, I began thinking about the man who waited by the pool of Bethesda for thirty-eight years for someone to help him get into the pool and be healed. I read the passage, John 5:1-8, to my friend, and I asked her to picture herself lying there by the pool, struggling with her own desire to be healed. Then I asked her to imagine Jesus approaching her. How would she feel? What might Jesus say to her? How would she respond to Jesus? By entering into this story in Scripture, my friend was able to experience God's love in a new way in her own situation. The Spirit touched her life in a quiet way, but one as real as the way Jesus touched the lame man. The Spirit's touch was personal and unique, well suited to her particular needs.

What one person experiences through imaginative reading and what another experiences may be quite different. Some time after I read the story from John 5 to my friend, I found the Spirit of God bringing it up in my own devotions. (It often happens to me that the conversations I have with directees come around again in my own life.) I had been praying about a number of relational entanglements that were draining life and energy from me. As I prayed, I talked with God about all the reasons these entanglements had gone on for so long and why I couldn't do anything about them. The passage in John came to mind. Reading the passage for myself this time, I was struck by Jesus' words to the ill man. Jesus said, "Stand up, take your mat and walk." These were familiar words to me. But this time, I heard the Spirit say to me, "Just walk!" And with that command came an invitation to let go of my need to figure things out and instead "just walk." All that week, when I was tempted to spiral back down into the entanglements of the relationship, I heard, "Just walk!" *Just get going. Live as though you're healed. Don't lie there anymore.* Those words seemed to guard my heart all week.

SCRIPTURE IN GROUP SPIRITUAL DIRECTION

How, then, might we experience all of this in group spiritual direction? As always, this will look different for different groups. And within any group there may be a variety of ways to view Scripture. It's also important to note that while references to Scripture passages may be appropriate in some situations, it's probably not realistic to expect the directee to engage deeply and personally with Scripture during the group spiritual direction session. However, with those cautions, let me say that transformational reading of Scripture can be a very, very valuable experience in a group setting. There are several ways this might happen.

Ahead of time. The first place transformational reading of Scripture can benefit group spiritual direction is actually outside the session, before the group meets. When members of the group have the habit of listening to God—in Scripture and in all aspects of life—they are much better equipped to listen to the directee with humble, welcoming attitudes. Also, the more steeped the members of the group are in the Word of God, the better equipped they are to contribute a truthful, helpful perspective to the discussion. And the more familiar they are with Scripture, the more equipped they are to draw from actual Bible passages when that's appropriate. So, then, one of the first gifts we can give to each other in group spiritual direction is to make it a habit to experience transformational reading of Scripture ourselves.

Lectio divina. Another way for a group to receive the benefits of transformational reading is for all the members of the group to select and read the same passage in a lectio divina fashion before they arrive for the meeting. Each member can take personal notes on some part of the passage as they read and then apply it to their own lives. Then when the group meets, before the directee presents, the facilitator can ask the members of the group to give a one- or two-minute summary of their own lectio experiences with the selected passage. In this case, it will be the facilitator's responsibility to make sure that the members share briefly, allowing plenty of time for the directee to present. If the group decides to commit to this kind of lectio experience, the person presenting as directee can be the last to share, and can start his or her presentation with the lectio sharing. Sometimes this helps a hesitant directee get started.

Reading Scripture to begin. Some groups choose to simply read a passage of Scripture to start out their time together. This is usually read slowly and quietly by the facilitator. Often only a few verses are read, and some or all of them may be read more than once, interspersed with times of silence.

Guided meditations. In our own church experience with group spiritual direction, we found that a good way to include transformational reading of Scripture was to start with a guided meditation. Several groups met the same evening, so we all gathered together at the beginning and I led a guided meditation for everyone. We allowed an hour and a half for the whole session, which gave us time to do this at the start. It became an opportunity for the group to gather, quiet down and listen to the Word of God together. The gathering and the meditation took about twenty minutes, and then we broke into small groups. Some of the groups chose to share their experiences during the guided meditations, but there was no pressure to do so. That left us with about an hour for the group spiritual direction time. Usually this meant that only one person could be the directee each time, though occasionally two people had the opportunity to present something from their own lives.

Using guided meditation in this way was so helpful in our own church's experience of group spiritual direction that I have included a number of guided meditations in appendix two. These meditations need not be done in order, or ahead of time, and there are no right or wrong answers. Each one simply provides a vehicle for people to enter into a passage from the Bible and seek to experience God's love in a personal, practical way, in light of that particular passage.

A creative experience. One of the things I love about spiritual direction is that it isn't a one-size-fits-all experience. This is especially true with group spiritual direction. All of these suggestions for using transformational reading in group direction need to be adapted for your own group. Different groups have different levels of maturity as well as different levels of familiarity with spiritual direction. With careful guidance and leadership, each group can participate in creating the schedule that fits its needs. The important thing is that when we come together for group direction, we do so with the intent of giving each other the opportunity to exprience love and grace, whether it is through Scripture or through the parables of our lives.

8

SIN, CONVICTION
AND CONFESSION

𝕯

Sin is considered by some to be the *S* word that is not to be mentioned in polite conversation. I can understand that. Even though I know deep within my being that the Bible is right in reminding me that I am indeed a sinner, I wish it weren't true! We shy away from the concept of sin because it gets pretty close to home. When a business acquaintance of mine was arrested for financial fraud, I was more comfortable thinking of his compulsive lying as a sickness than as sin. Even though his embezzlement was a crime as well as a sin, I did not want to think of him as a sinner. Likewise, I would rather call myself sick than sinful; calling sin a sickness sounds better, even though it isn't as accurate. But these semantic games miss the point.

If we dismiss sin as the *S* word, we also dismiss the instruction of Jesus and the teaching of the Bible. Jesus said, "I have come to call not the righteous but sinners" (Matthew 9:13). He taught us to pray, "Forgive us our sins" (Luke 11:4). Later Paul wrote to the church in Rome, "All have sinned and fall short of the glory of God" (Romans 3:23). As we think about spiritual direction, we cannot ignore sin.

But we can face the reality of sin with the reality of love and grace.

CONVICTION

A common misunderstanding of spiritual direction is that the director points out the sins of the directee. Some people even seem to want that to happen. Someone said to a friend of mine, "My spiritual director really nailed me on that one," and she seemed pleased about being "nailed." Since I happened to have been the spiritual director she was talking about, I wondered how she felt I had "nailed" her! That's not my picture of spiritual direction. If it were, I would not be motivated to make very many appointments with my own spiritual director. Nor would the idea of going to group spiritual direction be very endearing, if it meant I might be called upon to expose my sinful behavior to the whole group.

To set the record straight, spiritual direction is *not* about pointing out sin to people. That is the job of the Holy Spirit. Jesus said that the Spirit would "convict the world of guilt in regard to sin and righteousness and judgment" (John 16:8 NIV). The apostle Paul had this to say about sin and judgment: "I do not even judge myself. My conscience is clear, but that does not make me innocent. It is the Lord who judges me" (1 Corinthians 4:4 NIV). When I meet with someone for spiritual direction, it's not my job to point out sin. It's my job to do all that I can to create an environment where the directee can hear from God, whether it be about sin or about something else. The same thing is true in group spiritual direction. Our job is to be present to each other, so that each time one of us is the directee, we can listen to the Holy Spirit, whether the Spirit is convicting, forgiving or encouraging.

This takes a tremendous burden off of us as we listen to one another. We are not responsible for pointing out mistakes, inaccurate perspectives or sinful behavior. We need only to listen in and for truth and grace. When, through our listening, the Spirit of God convicts, it is always in the context of the good news of the gospel of grace. Jesus said that the Holy Spirit, who does indeed convict us of sin, is also our Advocate (John 16:7), someone who is on our side, not out to get us. And when Paul talked about the judgment of God, he said that God "will bring to light what is hidden in darkness and will expose the motives of men's hearts. At that time each will receive his *praise* from God" (1 Corinthians 4:5 NIV, emphasis mine). Praise? I thought conviction and judgment were about punishment, but here Paul is saying that when we're judged by God we'll be praised. Amazing. Perhaps this is why God does not give us the job of pointing out sin; we don't understand how to do it the way the Spirit does.

SO WHAT DO WE DO WITH SIN?

In spiritual direction, then, what do we do when we're faced with sinful behavior? We will sometimes listen to people describe attitudes and behavior that sound sinful, at least to us. What do we do with that? Paul asks a similar question in Romans 6 after his lengthy discourse on forgiveness: "What then are we to say? Should we continue in sin in order that grace may abound?" (v. 1). We might ask, "What then are we to say? In spiritual direction are we to disregard sin?" I would say with Paul, "By no means! How can we who died to sin go on living in it?" (Romans 6:2). If spiritual direction is a tool for deepening our communion with God, then we cannot ignore sin. But how do we approach the reality of sin in our own lives and in the lives of those we listen to without trampling down the shy, tender spirit within? How can we listen to one another in a way that reflects Jesus when he said: "He will not break a bruised reed / or quench a smoldering wick" (Matthew 12:20)?

It helps to remember that sin is not primarily about premeditated actions, like embezzlement. Sin is rooted in the attitude behind the action. It is the attitude in all human beings that causes us to think *we are in charge*. My friend who embezzled probably decided at some point that he was in charge of getting all the money he thought he needed. I am not an embezzler, but I do struggle with the temptation to think that I am in charge. I may act as though I am in charge of my life by rigidly planning my day without allowing any places for God to intervene. "I need to make this happen. And I *will* do it." When I look to myself and not to God to give me what I need, then I'm tempted to sin in my attitude and sometimes in my actions. Sin is rooted in a conscious or an unconscious disbelief in God's sovereign love. We sin because we disbelieve the truth of God and we believe the lies of Satan.

The Lies Behind Our Sin

The lies of Satan undermine our faith in several ways. First, Satan's lies challenge the truth of God's Word. In the account of the first sin (Genesis 3:1-10), Satan comes to Eve in the form of a serpent. Remember that Satan is "the deceiver of the whole world" (Revelation 12:9), "a liar and the father of lies" (John 8:44). His first question to Eve reflects his deceit: "Did God say, 'You shall not eat from any tree in the garden'?" (Genesis 3:1). Notice that Satan's challenge was based on a half-truth. God did not say Adam and Eve could not eat from *any* tree, but that they could not eat from the tree of the knowledge of good and evil (Genesis 2:16-17). Satan's lies are often based on half-truths, and they often start with the challenge, "Did God really say . . . ?" "Did God really say, 'You are precious in my sight, and honored, and I love you'?" (Isaiah 43:4). "Did God really say that the Holy Spirit would 'guide you into all truth'?" (John 16:13). "Did God really say that the Spirit of Jesus lives in us?" (Galatians 2:20). Satan asks questions like this all the time. The temptation to disbelieve the words of God is still with us.

And, like Eve, we are still tempted to respond not with the truth, but with a twisting of the truth. Like Eve, we are tempted to make obedience more difficult than it is. Eve answered the serpent, "We may eat of the fruit of the trees in the garden; but God said, 'You shall not eat of the fruit of the tree that is in the middle of the garden, nor shall you touch it, or you shall die'" (Genesis 3:3). Actually, God didn't say anything about touching the tree. Eve added something to God's words. Her twisting of God's words reminds me of the temptation I face in my own life to do the same thing. I'm tempted to think, *God loves me, but God would love me even more if I prayed better, or if I read the Bible more, or if I were a better person.* The serpent doesn't even bother responding to Eve's addition to God's command. He goes right for the jugular, with a blatant contradiction of God's words: "You will not die" (Genesis 3:4). In our own spiritual journeys we experience the same temptations to add to God's words or to blatantly contradict them.

Since we face temptations like this every day, it's something that will come up again and again in spiritual direction. This is why we need one another. I wonder what would have happened if Adam had come along and talked with Eve about what was going on. We'll never know what might have happened, because Adam didn't show up in the midst of Eve's temptation. But in the ministry of spiritual direction, we have a vehicle where we can be with each other and ask one another about the truth of what God is really saying in our lives.

I had been meeting with Liz for several months. One day she told me about this lingering guilt she felt over a minor mistake she had made years earlier. After she described what had happened, I asked her to be quiet for a moment and see if she had a sense of how God responded to her mistake. She said, "God told me to be more careful." Because I knew she was a very caring and careful person and that she lived with a lot of fear, I asked her to return to a time of quiet and continue to listen to God. This time her sense was that God understood, extended mercy and welcomed her into a loving embrace. For Liz, obedience to God meant never making mistakes. Like

Eve, she complicated God's desire for her and she faced the temptation to contradict God's grace and mercy. By talking about what she
thought was sin, Liz was able to find freedom from a weight of guilt.
She had been living with a voice inside that was saying, "Be careful!
Be careful! Be careful!" In truth, the Spirit of God wanted to say to
her, "Be loved! Be loved! Be loved!"

REACHING BEYOND OUR LIMITS

Another way human beings continue to be like Adam and Eve is in
our propensity to reach beyond God's provisions for us, including the
limitations he sets. God gave Adam and Eve a beautiful place to live,
interesting work to do and provision for all that they needed, from
food to companionship. The only thing they didn't have was permission to eat from the tree of the knowledge of good and evil. Scholars
debate the meaning of that tree, but one thing is clear: Adam and
Eve could not have it all. When they reached out to eat from that one
tree, they were saying to God that they would not accept the limitations God put in their lives. We have continued to do that ever since.
Our temptations are not connected with trees and fruit, but they are
rooted in the same desire to be more, have more or do more than
God has given us. We might, for instance, believe that we would be
happier if we had different talents, more money, different friends or
a different job. We're tempted to think that where God has placed us
is not good enough or what God has given us is not good enough.
We want more. We want to be in charge. Like Adam and Eve, we
face the temptation to be Creator rather than creatures.

This is a very alluring temptation. Notice that Eve looked at the
fruit of the forbidden tree and saw that it was beautiful and looked
tasty, and to top it off, the serpent said it would make her as wise as
God. What's not to like about something so good? Eve succumbed.
And ever since, human beings have been seeking out things that
look good, promise satisfaction and appeal to our desire to be in

control. Specifically, we face the temptation to do what only God can do: to determine the difference between good and evil, to be so capable that we can fix anything and so wise that we can understand everything.

These temptations come up again and again in our lives and in spiritual direction. Our job as companions to each other is not to chastise one another for our stupidity in believing Satan's lies. It is rather to lovingly support each other as we try to resist these difficult temptations.

Imagine for a moment a group meeting for spiritual direction with a businessman, a schoolteacher, a mother and a college student. Each of these four people faces a unique version of Adam and Eve's temptation to reach beyond the limits God gives us. The businessman might be tempted to believe that making money for the company justifies neglecting his children. The schoolteacher might carry the weight of believing she alone must solve all the problems of her students. The mother might be tempted to believe that every success or failure in her children reflects her parenting ability. And the college student may struggle with the fear that one bad grade will jeopardize his career path. All of these people are tempted to believe the lie that we do indeed know all that can be known about good and evil, that we are as wise as God, and that our destiny is in our own hands. As this group meets for spiritual direction, they can encourage each other to resist the temptation to disbelieve, and provide a loving environment where belief in God's love, mercy and provision become a daily experience.

THE TEMPTATION TO HIDE

The consequence of Adam and Eve's disbelief and twisting of God's Word is seen in the next event in the Genesis account. After they ate from the tree, Adam and Eve ran away. When God came looking for them, they were hiding. Adam said to God, "I heard the sound of you in the garden, and I was afraid, because I was naked; and I hid myself" (Genesis 3:10). Sin has that effect in our lives. It makes us feel spiritually naked. We hide not only from God but also from each other. In an effort to cover our spiritual nakedness we spend a great deal of energy trying to look good. We are afraid that if people knew who we really were on the inside of our souls, they wouldn't like us or think very highly of us. Like Adam and Eve, we hide.

This is one of the reasons that spiritual direction is a scary and a wonderful experience. Because it is a safe place where we have already agreed not to condemn one another, it is one place in our lives where we can be honest about our struggles with temptation. But this is a little scary. It may mean coming out of the bushes. In fact, in spiritual direction we ask one another, as God asked Adam and Eve, "Where are you?" Where are you today, in your spiritual life? If we respond to that question thoughtfully and truthfully, we will probably have to venture out from some of the bushes where we've been hiding. But it is worth it. I have found over the years that when I take that risk, I am strengthened to face temptations, and I begin to heal from the devastating effects of sin in my life.

CONFESSION

Spiritual direction is a place where I can confess my sins (James 5:16). In the broadest sense, to confess means to acknowledge the truth about something. When I "confess" my sins, I acknowledge the truth that I have believed lies, I have twisted truth, and I have gone beyond the truth of the limitations God has given me. More specifically, for me this means acknowledging that sometimes I don't believe God's love. It means acknowledging that often I want to fix other people's problems. It means admitting that I'm jealous of someone else's gifts or that I wish God had made me differently. When I confess my sins, I receive God's forgiveness. What has been hidden in the darkness of my heart is brought out into the light, and "darkness did not overcome it" (John 1:5). This is not just good news; this is great news! We don't need to fear that sin will win in the end. The darkness of our sin will not overwhelm the light of God's love in our souls.

Confession brings us to a place of light and forgiveness. It is also the first step toward transformation—which is what spiritual direction is all about. Psychologists tell us that self-awareness is 90 percent of change. So I need, first of all, to be aware of the particular temptations I face as a sinful human being. Awareness is the way we change direction. God's Spirit may lead us to make significant changes in our attitudes and behavior, but without awareness, change will not happen. Confession is the expression of awareness.

Confession in group spiritual direction can be hard and sometimes awkward, but it can bring God's grace in new ways to our lives. Ralph was a new participant in our church's group spiritual direction sessions. When it was his turn to present as directee, he started out by saying, "I love my wife, but I'm struggling with lustful thoughts toward other women." The group responded with an awkward silence and then rallied to invite Ralph to talk more. As he "confessed" his struggle, he relaxed. In response to the group's questions and interaction, he began to see that his struggle was not sin but temptation. And he was resisting the temptation. There was probably no other place in the church (except the privacy of the pastor's office) where Ralph could dialogue about such a personal experience. By the end of the session, Ralph's demeanor revealed his experience of grace. With a smile of relief he said, "Now I get what spiritual direction is about."

Does this mean that when we meet in group spiritual direction, we need to tell our friends all about our temptations and our sins? Probably not. Confession may be verbal, but more likely it will be a quiet admission to God about something that comes to our awareness as we're meeting with friends in a safe and loving place. As we engage in presenting something from our own lives and as we listen to others presenting, we're in constant communication with the Holy Spirit of God. Sometimes we may sense our spirits saying to God, "Forgive me for I have sinned." When that happens, we can remember that "if we confess our sins, he who is faithful and just will forgive us our sins and cleanse us from all unrighteousness" (1 John 1:9). As we are forgiven, we will begin to be transformed.

THE FINAL CHAPTER FOR SIN

At the end of the Bible, in the book of Revelation, we see how the sin of Adam and Eve is finally resolved. The love and grace of God, manifested in Jesus, will be celebrated in the new heaven and the new earth. John wrote in Revelation,

> See, the home of God is among mortals.
> He will dwell with them;
> they will be his peoples,
> and God himself will be with them;
> he will wipe every tear from their eyes.
> Death will be no more;
> mourning and crying and pain will be no more,
> for the first things have passed away. (Revelation 21:3-4)

I can hardly imagine God wiping the tears from my eyes. I can hardly imagine life without mourning, pain and sin. This is because we have not come to the final chapter yet. It is as though we are living in the Saturday between Good Friday and Easter. Sin has been conquered on the cross, but the final defeat of sin is still in process. Until then we will face daily temptations to sin. We desperately need one another to help us navigate this journey. In spiritual direction we find friends and spiritual companions who, in the name of Jesus, stay with us in this painful struggle against temptation and sin and remind us that God does indeed dwell among us. As we companion one another on this journey, we experience God's presence and love.

9

SHARING THE
JOURNEY OF PRAYER

⌓

Rebecca was scheduled to present one evening in our spiritual direction group at church. She began by saying, "Tonight I want to talk about my prayer life." Then she told us how it was changing, what she liked and didn't like about it, and the questions she had about her own ways of praying. The group listened, affirmed and asked questions to help her process her experience. She seemed encouraged. But in all honesty, it was one of those experiences of group spiritual direction where I wondered if anything had "happened."

Reflecting back on the time, I realized that something astounding had happened: Rebecca had been given the opportunity to talk with several other people about prayer—one of the most intimate and mysterious experiences of life. As she talked about how she prayed, her prayer life became more real and more alive for her. She was no longer alone in this deeply personal part of her relationship with God. Furthermore, as she shared about her experiences in prayer and received the companionship of others, she opened herself to more of the companionship of God.

PRAYER IS LOVE

St. Augustine said the "true, whole prayer is nothing but love." The subtitle of Richard Foster's book on prayer is *Finding the Heart's True Home*. Praying, then, is like coming home to a loving God. In my own life, I like to think of prayer as the experience of running into the arms of God, who is waiting for me just as the father waited for the prodigal son (Luke 15:11-24). Michael Casey says that "prayer is not just dialogue; it is the first stage of surrender." When I pray, I am surrendering myself to the love of God.

We often think of prayer as something we *do* or *say*. "I prayed," we tell our friends, "that God would heal [or help, or give me something] and God answered my prayers." There is nothing wrong with praying that God will help us and heal us, but this description of prayer misses the point. It sounds like we're in charge, like we make something happen by praying. We give God instructions. This is not what prayer is really about. If, as Augustine said, prayer is nothing but love, then when we pray, we are allowing ourselves to be loved by God and we open ourselves to experience and to reflect that love in whatever way it's manifested. Prayer is not something we do to control life, just as love is not something we control. Love is something we *receive* and we *give*. Prayer, then, is a gift we receive from God that allows us to participate in the work of love which God is doing in our lives and in the world.

Spiritual direction is all about our relationship with God. Prayer is at the heart of that relationship. The more we can learn about prayer, the more equipped we'll be to companion others in their prayer experiences. In this chapter, then, we'll look at prayer in light of Scripture, our daily lives and our spiritual journey.

PRAYER AND SCRIPTURE

People who are experienced in prayer often notice that their prayers are deeply rooted in Scripture. When they pray, they pray Scripture.

Calvin Miller says that "the key in all of our Scripture praying is to let the Word become the mode of our transport. . . . When we are reading the Scripture, the border between Scripture and prayer becomes so thin that they meld into each other and we are united with God." We do this when we read slowly, as in lectio divina. We do this when we stop our reading and muse on a truth we see in Scripture. We do this when we carry a verse or two in our minds and hearts throughout the day. And we do this when we use the words of Scripture to pray our own prayers.

I have found that praying the Scriptures is a very helpful way to express my inner desires when they are hidden by stress, defeat or anxiety. At one difficult time in my life, all I could do was pray the prayer of Job: "Though he slay me, yet will I hope in him" (Job 13:15 NIV). That may have been a little dramatic, but praying those words helped me hope. Another time Psalm 23:4 became my prayer: "Even though I walk through the valley of the shadow of death . . ." As I prayed this, the operative word for me was *through*. I prayed that God would lead me through the valley of the death of my expectations for my life at that time, that I would make it through the changes which were happening in my circumstances, and that God would sustain me and strengthen me to do what needed to be done as I walked through the valley. On more ordinary days, I often pray that God will "carry me" as God promised through the prophet Isaiah that he would carry the Israelites (Isaiah 46:3). When Scripture becomes my prayer, I am drawn closer to God, the author of all truth.

When we meet together in group spiritual direction, Scripture provides a foundation for our conversations about prayer, whether this foundation is verbalized or not. Most of the time we'll just listen, and hear how others have prayed and experienced Scripture in their own lives. Occasionally, we may suggest something from Scripture ourselves, but we do this tentatively and lovingly. In a recent group experience, during one of the times of silence, words of Scripture came to my mind with unusual clarity. After the silence, I mentioned the words to the person presenting. But I didn't elaborate or pontificate on them. I just offered them to her. If those words turned out to be a way for her to pray about what she had presented, I'm grateful. I didn't need to give her my application of the truth of that Scripture. That's the job of the Holy Spirit, who gives us truth, in love, at the moment we can hear it.

EXAMINING OUR DAILY LIVES

Ignatius, who was known for his advice on discernment, suggested a discipline which can also be a form of prayer: the daily examen. This is not, as I first thought, a time to think and pray about all of our sins. It is, rather, a way to reflect on our day, in dialogue with God. After we take a minute or two to quiet our hearts and focus our attention, we think back over the last day or two. Then, in the presence of God, we notice the times when we felt the closest to our loving Father. These may be times when we felt joy or freedom or a deep sense of God's presence. They may even be times when we felt conviction—the conviction that comes with the invitation to return to God's love. Then we notice the times when we felt most distant from God, such as times when we felt anxious or discouraged or tied up in knots. In these moments we might have felt that the weight of the world, or at least our own lives, sat squarely on our own shoulders.

This is not a prayer of request or commentary. In this prayer experience, we simply notice. It is a prayer of relationship. It is sharing our day with the Holy Spirit of Love. After we pray this way, we may want to move into confession, petition or intercession. But first of all we look "with the eyes of [our] heart" (Ephesians 1:18) to see our lives as God sees them.

Some people have found that this prayer of examen is a good way to begin group spiritual direction. This is especially helpful in a setting where people are not used to thinking of God intersecting their lives in intimate ways. When the group gathers, allowing a brief time for this reflective prayer can be a good way to quiet down before the presenter begins. This can remain a personal experience, or it could lead to a time of brief sharing.

PRAYER ON THE JOURNEY

Prayer is an integral part of our spiritual journey. It is the essence of our communion with God. Sometimes our prayers are verbal, sometimes they're silent. Sometimes we can describe our prayer life, sometimes it's beyond description. Sometimes we seem to initiate our prayers, and sometimes it seems as though God speaks to us first.

Brendan, the Celtic pilgrim, was known for his seafaring journeys, undertaken out of spiritual longing and obedience. Calvin Miller wrote this about Brendan:

> When the wind died and the sail hung limp, the men rowed, though they knew not where. Finally Brendan ordered the fatigued rowers to stop. He cried, "God is our helper. He is our navigator and helmsman, and he shall guide us. Pull in the oars and the rudder. Spread the sail and let God do as he wishes with his servants and their boat."

Sometimes as we pray, we sense that the Spirit is inviting us to stop our hard rowing, pull in the oars and let God guide the boat. We need to let go. Letting go of our own agenda does not mean that it won't happen, or that it is necessarily contrary to the will of God. It just means that we stop trying so hard. We receive, rather than make something happen. We let God guide the boat. This sense of letting go is at the heart of prayer.

Thomas Keating, well known for his teaching and writing about prayer, suggests that there are three desires we need to let go of: our desire for control and power; our desire for affection, esteem and approval; and our desire for security and survival. In all honesty, when I read that list, my first response was, "That will never happen!" And many times since then, as I have prayed "I let go of my desire for control, affection and security," I find myself having this one-way conversation with God:

"Well, actually, I don't let go at all."
"But I want to."
"Well, I sort of want to."
"God, help me want to."

The experience of letting go, I have found, is not something for the faint-hearted in prayer. It is not something we learn once and then live out of ever-after. It is, rather, the syntax of our ongoing spiritual journey. Over and over again we remember that God invites us to let go. Jesus, the God of the universe, is *in our boat.* (Remember the story in Mark 4:35-41.) When we pray, sometimes God invites us to pull in the oars, spread the sails and let God take us where he wills.

Silent Prayer

When we "pull in our oars," we may find that we have nothing else to say. This reflects the experience of Paul that he described in his letter to the church at Rome. He wrote that "the Spirit helps us in our weakness; for we do not know how to pray as we ought, but that very Spirit intercedes with sighs too deep for words" (Romans 8:26). I like to think that when I am silent in prayer, the Holy Spirit is interceding for me "according to the will of God" (Romans 8:27).

In writing about silent prayer, Thomas Keating describes centering prayer, which is the experience of being intentionally silent before God. Keating suggests that when we pray in silence, we use no words, we do not dwell on any thoughts, and we do not follow the wanderings of our minds. It is, as he says, like taking a vacation from ourselves. Keating recommends that we intentionally do this for twenty minutes twice a day. Many people have found that this discipline deepens their relationship with God immensely.

Other people are helped just by remembering that silence, as well as words, can be prayer. "For God alone my soul waits in silence," the psalmist wrote (Psalm 62:1). If prayer is nothing but love, then that love can be expressed silently or with words.

SPIRITUAL DIRECTION AS PRAYER

When we meet in group spiritual direction, we want to encourage each other to grow in whatever ways the Spirit leads us to pray. In some literature, spiritual direction is actually called prayer, since it's a coming together in the presence of one another to *listen* to God, and then, as we talk with one another and sit in times of silence, it offers time to *talk* to God. Walter Wangerin says that in prayer, we talk and God listens. Then God talks and we listen. In group direction, we talk and we listen.

This is what happened when Elizabeth presented in her group. She chose to talk about how sad she was that a close friend, Lynn, was moving away, and that she feared she was too attached to Lynn. Elizabeth talked and God listened. Elizabeth's friends, in whom the Spirit dwells, also listened. Then they entered a brief time of silence for members of the group to listen to God. After that the group listened again to Elizabeth and affirmed her love for Lynn. Members of the group observed that God loved Lynn even more than Elizabeth did. The response of the group completed the circle of prayer because through their support, God talked and Elizabeth listened. In this way, the group experience was indeed prayer.

BECOMING PRAY-ERS

Early in our experience of parenting, my husband and I were drawn to a quote we saw on a seminary bulletin board: "The best thing a father can do for his children is to love their mother." Even as young parents, we had an inkling that this was true. In a similar way, one of the best things we can do to become better spiritual companions of others is to seek to deepen our own prayer lives and relationship with God. As we grow closer and more in love with our heavenly Father, we are more inclined and better equipped to love God's children. In group spiritual direction, we can do this by offering to one another what Rebecca and Elizabeth's groups offered to them: against the background of our own love for God, we listen, support and reflect back what we hear as someone describes his or her own prayer life.

Because we ourselves are pray-ers, we know the many questions prayer brings and can include in our group spiritual direction conversations gentle and nonjudgmental questions about prayer such as

- What is it like for you when you pray about this situation you're presenting?

- How has prayer been helpful to you in the past?

- What are some new ways you might like to experience God in prayer?

As with many of the questions we ask, the words are not as important as asking the question in an inviting, compassionate way.

Prayer in Group Spiritual Direction

Sometimes groups can offer to pray for the person presenting at the end of their presentation, but it's important to ask the presenter if that sounds like a good idea. Also, some people in the group may not feel comfortable praying out loud, so it might be good to suggest silent prayer, with the group leader closing either with the Lord's Prayer or a simple "Amen." Alternately, one person could volunteer to pray on behalf of the whole group.

If your group chooses to pray aloud, remember that the purpose of prayer is to bring your friend's needs to God, not to talk to your friend about what he or she needs to do. I have been in groups where people have prayed, "God help this friend do [or believe, or think] such-and-such." When that happens, prayer can sound a lot like preaching—which is not part of spiritual direction. But even with that precaution, prayer can be a truly meaningful group experience. Every group will need to come to their own way of praying.

In his book *The Path of Celtic Prayer,* Calvin Miller tells another story about Brendan that gives some hints for us in approaching prayer in group direction. In this particular story, the monks who were with Brendan on his sea journey saw land in the distance.

> Then the monks were filled with joy and began to row as quickly as they could. When [Brendan] saw this, he said: "Don't row so hard, or you will exhaust yourselves. Is almighty God not the helmsman and captain of our ship? Do not strain yourselves, since he guides us where he will."

This is a metaphor for me of what can happen on our prayer journey. We can have a prayer experience that seems like we have "arrived," or at least come to some milestone that is meaningful to us. It is, metaphorically, as though we are in a ship and we see land. Naturally, we want to row hard and take everyone with us! But once again, Brendan reminds me that it may be better to pull in the oars and let God guide us all.

In meeting together for group spiritual direction, we have agreed to get into the same boat. But the landscape we are heading toward, especially in prayer, will look a little different for all of us. The invitation we give to one another is to be in the boat together, but not necessarily to row harder and harder. Instead of rowing we are invited to pray, alone or together, and see where God guides us.

TEMPERAMENT AND
HOW WE COMMUNICATE

✑

One of the most fundamental realities of spiritual growth is that we all grow at different rates and in different ways. In group spiritual direction this means that each person in the group is different from all the other people, and thus the directee—the person presenting— is uniquely different from everyone else. The more we know about our differences, the more equipped we are to listen to the presenter with openness and grace.

The first summer my husband and I moved to the Chicago area, we spent a day wandering around Navy Pier, one of the great tourist attractions of our new city. When we got there, I was overwhelmed by the huge baskets and planters of flowers. The geraniums, mari- golds and day lilies were brilliant in the sun. We walked to the end of the pier and then turned the corner to walk back along the other side. On this new side, large, overflowing planters of impatiens were brilliant in the shade. Tears came to my eyes: the gardeners at Navy Pier treated the flowers better than we human beings treat each other. The gardeners knew that some flowers grow better in

the shade than in the sun. Some tolerate heat. Others will die when
the temperature rises. Flowers, like people, need different environ-
ments in order to flourish. Sometimes we forget that with our fellow human beings.

The problem with our forgetfulness is that it causes us to assume
that all people are like we ourselves are. Those who like parties are
surprised that others don't. Those who like to read are surprised by
people who don't even have a library card. Those who love the unexpected can't understand people who want to plan everything out.
Those who like church services are amazed that some people don't.
We could go on and on. It seems so obvious. But we forget. This is
why it is helpful to have tools, or systems, which give names to our
differences.

MYERS-BRIGGS TYPE INDICATOR®

One of the more popular tools is the Myers-Briggs Type Indicator
(MBTI). This system defines psychological differences in sixteen different categories. The simplest presentation of this comes as a chart
with sixteen boxes. I do *not* like putting people in boxes, but I do
like Myers-Briggs immensely. The reason I like it is that I've found
that without at least sixteen boxes, I have only one—my own box.
And *my* box is always the right one. Since I know in my better moments that my way is not the only way, I find it helpful to be given
at least fifteen more "boxes" or perspectives to help me understand
and encourage people who are different from me.

MBTI is a description of our natural preferences, based on four
categories which grew out of the work of Carl Jung and was later
popularized by Isabel Myers and Katharine Briggs in the 1950s. The
four categories are (1) how we are energized, (2) how we perceive
the world around us, (3) how we make decisions and (4) how we live
out these preferences. MBTI observes these categories but does not
evaluate or judge them. Our preferences are as deeply rooted in us

as our preference to write with our left or right hand. I teach workshops on Myers-Briggs, and I often start with an exercise suggested by MBTI literature. First I ask everyone in the group to write their name on a piece of paper, as though they are signing a check. Then I ask them to put the pen in the other hand and write their name again. At the second writing, the room fills with sounds of chuckling, groans of embarrassment and sighs of frustration. Then I ask the group to tell me how they felt when they wrote their name with their nonpreferred hand. I get responses like, "It was so hard." "It took longer." "I had to really think about it." "It made me feel childish." "I didn't like doing it."

By that time most people in the group have figured out that the name-writing exercise is a simple example of how difficult it is to do something we are not used to doing, something that is not our first-choice preference. The categories of MBTI give words to our preferences in areas of life that are much more important than the hand we use to write our signature. These preferences are equally ingrained in us, and without noticing, we will choose our "right hand" or our "left hand" every time. And if for some reason we cannot live according to our preferences, life will be more difficult for us.

It shouldn't surprise us that we're different from one another in our abilities, our likes and dislikes, and our preferences. But it does surprise us. If we're honest, most of us will admit that we naturally assume that our choices are the best—a good example of what everyone should choose. This has disastrous implications for the spiritual journey, where each individual is uniquely created by God. We are, each of us, "wonderfully made" (Psalm 139:14). All of us are created in the image of God the Creator (Genesis 1:27), but none of us reflects all of who God is. Together we reflect God in our variety of gifts, but even that reflection is made up of infinite variations. Embracing our differences is one way to praise God for divine creativity and infinite possibilities. Naming these differences is one way to em-

brace them. MBTI, then, is a helpful paradigm as we consider group
spiritual direction. It helps us identify the many different ways we
grow spiritually and the variety of experiences which nurture and
encourage us in our relationship with God. Let's take a look at this
paradigm of psychological preferences and then see how it can help
in group spiritual direction.

WHERE WE GET OUR ENERGY

The first category of the Myers-Briggs paradigm is Extroversion-
Introversion (E/I). This is the category that describes where we get our
energy: from our outer world or our inner world. Extroverts (about 75
percent of the population, according to most MBTI researchers) are
energized by their outer world. Being with other people, getting out
and about, talking things over with others, all give energy to extroverts. Introverts, on the other hand, are energized by being alone, by
musing in private about ideas, people and life. Being around a number of people actually drains energy away from introverts. Some people say, "It's not that introverts are party poopers, it's that the party
poops them." When an introvert says, "I'll have to think about that,"
it doesn't mean they are dismissing your idea. It just means that to do
justice to your idea they'll have to think about it when they're alone.
On the flip side, when an extrovert comes to a meeting and wants
to talk about an issue that was on the agenda well ahead of time, it
doesn't mean they didn't do their homework. It just means that they
are able to think best when they can talk about the issue.

Whether we prefer introversion or extroversion is going to make
a huge difference in our spiritual journeys. Extroverts will probably like conferences, church services and meetings, group prayer,
and group Bible study. Introverts will probably prefer "quiet times"
alone, private prayer, private Bible study, and lots of time to muse
and think. If they don't each understand this difference, extroverts
may say that the only way to grow spiritually is to come to meetings,

and introverts may say that the only way to grow is to take time to be alone!

This preference, interestingly, may change when we approach midlife. Because there are probably three times as many extroverts as introverts in our society, an introvert must learn extrovert skills in order to function well. But an extrovert can move into midlife never having had to develop introvert skills. At midlife they may find themselves saying, "I used to be an extrovert, but I think I'm becoming an introvert." This is because at midlife, we typically want to grow parts of ourselves that have been functioning only at a minimal level. So an extrovert at midlife may suddenly discover the joys of a quieter, more personal walk with God. Group spiritual direction provides a good stepping stone for extroverts who want to be able to talk through what is happening in their inner world.

WHAT WE TAKE IN FROM OUR WORLD

The next category of MBTI is Sensing-Intuitive (S/N). This is the category which describes how we perceive life, what things catch our attention, what information is important to us. Sensing people notice things with their five senses—seeing, hearing, touching, smelling and tasting. Intuitive people notice the unseen world by inference, by intuition and by making connections.

I am an intuitive type. My sister, however, is a sensing type. One evening we visited a small gift shop together. We were the only ones there except for the clerk. After almost an hour inside, we walked out to the street. My sister took a deep breath and said, "Whew. It's good to get away from her smoking." I said, "Oh, was she smoking? I didn't even notice. I just wondered why she was so sad." Two people, the same place, two different experiences. That's the way it is with sensing and intuitive people.

Again, this has large implications for our spiritual life. Intuitive people tend to find God through insights, imagination and unseen spiritual experiences. Sensing people, however, will often find God in what can be seen, in institutions and in practical expressions of their faith. In addition, intuitive people often like change while sensing people usually prefer things the way they are. Intuitive people may jump to conclusions, while sensing people prefer to go step by step. A church needs both kinds of people—those who see the reality of what is, and those who see what could be. But it takes grace and love for these two kinds of people to work together. Myers-Briggs provides a tool to give words to their preferences and to celebrate their differences.

This category of the MBTI paradigm is especially important in spiritual direction, where we are talking about the mysteries of God, about realities we cannot see. It is easy for intuitive types (like me) to make assumptions and intuitive leaps that leave sensing people shaking their heads. I had been meeting with a woman who is in the sensing category for several months. One of my frequent questions as she talked about her life was "Where do you see God in all of this?" That made perfect sense to me. How did she see God at work in the events of her life? Where did she see the influence of God's grace and guidance? But what she heard was "Where do you *see* God?" She thought I meant that she would physically see God. Fortunately my spiritual direction friend and I were able to clear up her misunderstanding and my miscommunication. And since God's truth is manifested in the senses as well as through things unseen and not felt, it is good that we have each other for companions on the journey.

HOW WE MAKE DECISIONS

The third MBTI category is the Thinking-Feeling (T/F) category and describes how we make decisions. Thinkers base their decisions on logic, cause and effect, and analytical reasoning. Feelers base their decisions on how the decision will affect the people involved and on value rather than logic. This is the only category that's influenced by gender. According to MBTI research, 60 percent of men are thinkers and 60 percent of women are feelers. But with both men and women, it is very important to remember that thinkers feel and feelers think. The category describes the bottom-line of decision making, not the ability of either type of person to think clearly or feel deeply. Hopefully all human beings do both of those!

I saw this play out in a real-life decision at one workshop I attended. Someone needed to make a decision about whether or not to lay off an employee. His department was divided about what to do. The problem was that the most likely candidate to be laid off was experiencing serious family problems, including a major illness. Some people in the department (probably the people in the feeling category of Myers-Briggs) said that the company should not even consider laying off this man whose wife had cancer. Other people in the department (probably those in the thinking category) said that the company needed to do what was best for the company and that it was only logical that this person should be the one to go. I don't know what decision was made, but my friend at the workshop seemed to be helped by understanding how temperament influences our decisions.

Groups meeting for spiritual direction will, of course, include thinkers and feelers. This means that the person presenting will have the opportunity to reflect on questions offered from both perspectives. It also means that members of the group will want to honor the preference of the presenter while trying to bring in a complete viewpoint of reality. Balancing these two ways of looking at life is an art, not a science. Sometimes we want to live according to the value judgments of feelers, and sometimes the logical viewpoint of thinkers is more appropriate. Processing our experiences with a group is one way to get that balance.

How We Live Our Lives

The fourth MBTI category is an interesting one. Myers-Briggs describes some people as Judgers (J) and some people as Perceivers (P), depending on our preferences about how to live our lives. People in the judging category like to plan ahead and finish their goals. People in the perceiving category like spontaneity and like to keep their options open. Judgers like to make life happen, while perceivers like to let life happen. Once again, however, the labels of MBTI categories are limited. Just because someone is a judger does not mean they're judgmental (although they may be). And perceivers can be judgmental about people who don't like to live life spontaneously. The important thing is not the label, as necessary as that is. What's key is the acknowledgment that we all approach our lives with different ideas about how to experience each day.

I once asked a group of people who worked together in a Christian service organization how each of them started their day and what expectations they had for a day. Those who were in the judging category said that they liked to plan out each day so that they would get the most out of it. Those in the perceiving category liked to let the day unfold. One man said, "I just like to see what the Spirit brings my way." Someone else in the judging category could have said, "I like to ask the Spirit to help me plan each hour."

This is a very subtle, very important category to understand. It not only influences our own spiritual journeys, it also affects what happens when we come together in community. Without embracing the truth that it is okay to be different, we may indeed be quick to judge each other. When we can celebrate our differences, we can experience the variety of ways the Holy Spirit may lead us. Sometimes the Spirit leads in ways that confirm the importance of doing things "decently and in order" (1 Corinthians 14:40). Other times the Spirit reminds us to "not worry about tomorrow, for tomorrow will worry about itself" (Matthew 6:34 NIV).

MBTI IN GROUP SPIRITUAL DIRECTION

One of the benefits of group spiritual direction is that we bump into people who look at life differently from us. In my own life, with my particular way of looking at things, I often run into dead ends. It is a gift to me to have others come along beside me and look at my life through different eyes. This is why the Myers-Briggs Type Indicator can be so helpful in group spiritual direction. It offers us a frame of reference for understanding and relating to people who are different from us. Let me suggest three specific ways we can appropriate MBTI in group spiritual direction: in self-awareness, in listening and in asking questions.

SELF-AWARENESS

Myers-Briggs, first and foremost, gives the gift of self-knowledge. Spiritual teachers say that we cannot know God unless we know ourselves, and we cannot know ourselves unless we know God. In his *Institutes of the Christian Religion,* John Calvin said that "nearly all wisdom we possess . . . consists of two parts: the knowledge of God and of ourselves." Our own spiritual growth will be limited by our blind spots. Where we do not know ourselves and where we are blind, we cannot see God's grace and love. Likewise, we will be limited by our blind spots in our ability to companion others on their spiritual journeys. MBTI helps us know ourselves. As we experience the ongoing revelation of ourselves, we experience the ever-continuing invitation to embrace God's grace. And as we embrace and are embraced by God's grace in our own lives, we are able to extend that invitation to others.

Let me give you a personal example. For most of my life, I came home from church tired and in a bad mood. I couldn't figure out why. I assumed something was wrong with me, and I felt guilty about it. Then I learned from MBTI that I am an introvert and that spending several hours at church on Sunday morning is exhausting. This bit of self-knowledge drew me closer to God because it freed me from spending so much time worrying about what I might be doing wrong. I believe that God created me and loves me as I am—an introvert who gets tired out in large groups. I still come home from church tired, but now I'm not in a bad mood. I just look forward to the quiet afternoon ahead!

Listening

Myers-Briggs also helps us listen. In group spiritual direction each person is listening carefully to one person who is talking about everyday life, the spiritual journey, relationships and events. With the help of MBTI as we listen, we can be alert to that person's preferences. In addition, we can set aside our own preferences, at least temporarily, in order to listen to how the Spirit might be leading our friend. C. S. Lewis wrote, "Each of the Redeemed shall forever know and praise some one aspect of the divine beauty better than any other creature can. . . . Each has something to tell all others—fresh and ever-fresh news of the 'My God' whom . . . all praise as 'Our God.'" With the help of Myers-Briggs, we can listen carefully for the unique way our friend knows and praises God.

The way we listen will be influenced by our MBTI preferences, as will the dynamics of the whole group. For example, in one spiritual direction group of four, there were two extroverts and two introverts. The two extroverts could not understand why the introverts didn't speak up more. Peter was especially quiet. But toward the end of almost every session, Peter had an insightful question or comment. His silence, the group learned, was not an empty silence but one filled with observation and wisdom. The extroverts, with their engaging conversation, tilled the soil for Pete's inner reflections. Together they helped each other listen for God.

Asking Questions

Finally, Myers-Briggs helps us know what questions to ask. We want to ask questions which will help the person presenting to identify his or her preferences and discern how the Spirit seems to be working in the context of those preferences: Is this an area of life where I'm being invited to live according to my preference? Or is this a time when I need to choose to do something which will be innately difficult for me? We cannot answer those questions unless we have some idea of what our preferences are. Below I offer some suggestions for questions we might ask in group spiritual direction as we listen and interact with the directee. These very general questions may provide a jumping-off point for self-awareness. Pick one or two which seem relevant to the issue the person is presenting.

To help determine a preference for extroversion or introversion:

- In what setting do you feel closest to God: when you're alone (as introverts do) or when you're with other people (as extroverts do)?

- Are you more likely to find your heart turning to God when you're in conversation with others or when you're by yourself?

To help determine a preference for sensing or intuiting information:

- What do you like best about your relationship with God: what you've already experienced (as sensors are likely to prefer) or the potential of what you could come to experience (as intuitives might prefer)?

- Do you like to think and talk about what you know to be true about the spiritual life or about the mysteries of the spiritual life?

To help determine a preference for thinking or feeling in decision making:

- If you have an important decision to make, do you find yourself focusing on the most logical conclusion (as thinkers will) or the one that will be the most helpful to the people involved (as feelers do)?

- Which do you enjoy more: analyzing a situation or considering the needs of the people affected by the situation?

To help determine a judging or perceiving approach to life:

- Are you more likely to be excited about finishing a project (as judgers are) or about exploring all the possible options in the project (as perceivers are)?

- Do you enjoy living your day with a schedule or without a schedule?

Asking questions like this in an open-ended way invites the person presenting in a spiritual direction group to identify and embrace their own preferences in life. In general, God's direction for us is synchronized with these preferences. On the occasions when God's love calls us to do something outside our preferences, it helps to admit that we are "writing with the other hand."

However God leads us in the circumstances of our daily lives—whether according to our preferences or not—God will be with us. We can remind each other of that.

11

DISCERNMENT
AMONG FRIENDS

꿈

The brochure our church uses to invite people to participate in group spiritual direction gives several reasons why someone might want to come. "You may want to seek spiritual direction," it reads, "if you long for a deeper sense of God's love in your life, if you feel your activities are more burdensome than life-giving, if you have questions about what you believe, if you struggle with feeling disconnected, fearful, or angry, or if you face an important decision or transition in your life." Most of these reasons have to do with discernment. How do we perceive God in our lives? How do we know what God wants for us? How do we make good choices on our spiritual journey? These are questions we ask throughout our lives. One of the main reasons I go to my own spiritual director is to be able to process these questions in each season of my life. And discernment is one of the main reasons people come to group spiritual direction. We long for an ongoing, dynamic relationship with God and we sense that sharing this quest with others will help us.

Since discernment is such a significant part of the spiritual direction process, it's important to look at what it is and how it happens. Discernment is not just about "finding God's will for my life." Discernment, according to author David Lonsdale, is the capacity to distinguish between two paths, "one leading to fullness of life in the love of God; the other leading in a direction that is ultimately dehumanizing and destructive." He adds that discernment is "one of the gifts which enables God's reign to be not only a dream but also a daily reality" and that it takes place in everyday life as well as in decisions about our future.

Thomas Green, another author well known for his insights about discernment, maintains that we must hold our discernment loosely. Faith (the conviction of things not seen, according to Hebrews 11:1) is always a part of discernment. Green says that discernment is always "tentative" because it is based on "conflicting and ambivalent" life situations, and that it "is not a way of short-circuiting faith; rather it is a way of choosing how to act in faith." Discernment, then, is not so much about certainty as it is about relating to God in ways that allow the Spirit of God to transform us into people who more and more instinctively walk in God's love.

Discernment is about paying attention to God at work in our lives. It's about testing the spirits (see 1 John 4:1) and coming to recognize when our choices are coming from the false self, the self controlled by our selfish egos, and when our choices are rooted in our true self, the self created by God and in the process of being transformed by love and grace.

Discernment also involves learning to respond to ourselves, to other people and to circumstances in ways that are consistent with God's purposes. It's not the same as problem solving. In discernment, we seek God and God's perspective about ourselves and the presenting situation or relationship. After discernment, we work through the logistics of whatever we have decided to do. We deal with any problems that arise, asking for God's help. The apostle Paul wrote that God is working in us, enabling us "to will and to work for his good pleasure" (Philippians 2:13). He gives us wisdom in the discernment process.

When we're meeting with others in group spiritual direction, there are several truths about discernment to keep in mind: First, God relates to us as adults. Second, God's desires for us mesh with the hopes and desires of our true selves. And third, effective discernment requires an open, waiting and willing spirit.

ADULT CHILDREN

Thomas Green says that "the God of the Judaeo-Christian tradition is, and wishes to be, neither a watchmaker nor a puppeteer but a father of adult children. His choice to relate to us in this way is the foundation of all Christian discernment." This explains a lot to me. As a young Christian, I thought that the watchmaker image was accurate—that "doing God's will" meant carefully fitting into the place God has for me, just as a watchmaker has a precise place for every part of the watch. Without realizing it, I lived as though Green's second analogy was also true—that God was in heaven moving people around like a puppeteer above the stage of life. Even today as an adult, I sometimes forget that God's desires for me are dynamic and alive, that God treats me as an adult, not as a puppet.

I understand a little more what this means when I think about my own desires for my adult children. When our children were small, I carefully guided them through the dangers of life: busy streets, things that choke, light plugs that can shock. But as they grew up, I gave them less and less guidance. Now that they have children of their own and are busy living their own lives, my role is primarily to love, support and affirm. According to the Bible, this is the way God relates to us. In his story of the prodigal son, Jesus says that God is like the father who lets his adult son go off and spend his inheritance and then welcomes this son back into the family (Luke 15:11-24).

The father in Jesus' story didn't impose his will on his son. He gave his son freedom. Then he welcomed his son home, even when the young man had made choices the father didn't want for him. In the same way, God is *always* standing in the road welcoming us, his adult children, back home.

The apostle Paul encouraged Christians to become adults in their faith. He wrote to the church in Ephesus, "We must no longer be children, tossed to and fro" (Ephesians 4:14). To the church in Corinth he wrote, "I could not speak to you as spiritual people, but rather as people of the flesh, as infants in Christ" (1 Corinthians 3:1). God wants us to grow up. And as we grow up, God relates to us as adults.

This, of course, has huge implications for discernment. In the same way that I don't phone my adult children and tell them what they should do for the day, so God allows us freedom and choice. And in the same way I'm delighted to see my children grow up, I believe God is delighted to see us grow up. Discernment is about learning to live as adult children of God, not getting all the instructions we needed when we were very young.

GOD'S DESIRES FOR US

Another important part of discernment is remembering that God's will for us is, to use a biblical word, *pleasant* (Psalm 16:6). This is a truth I needed to learn. Before I embraced the truth that God's will for me will be pleasant, I assumed that God wanted me to become a missionary. I went to missionary conferences. I answered many calls to be a missionary. But I struggled with the contradictions to that calling that I saw in myself. I don't travel well. I don't have the stamina that my missionary friends have, and I'm not as adaptable as I wish I were. But I assumed that none of that mattered to God. God would take me overseas whether I wanted to go or not.

I'm embarrassed now by this misunderstanding of God. But I

know I'm not alone. Many people assume that God's will is difficult and unpleasant. For people with this perspective, discernment
probably means trying to talk themselves into doing something they
really don't want to do. The possibility that God's desires for us will
correspond to our own deepest desires is a new thought for many
people. But if we assume that God's will is something we will not
like, then we'll be tempted to look for happiness on our own. David
Benner writes about this in *Sacred Companions:*

> Ignatius of Loyola suggests that sin is ultimately a refusal to
> believe that what God wants is my happiness and fulfillment.
> When I fail to believe this, I am tempted to sin—to take my
> life into my own hands, assuming that I am in the best posi-
> tion to determine what will lead to my happiness. As I become
> convinced that God wants nothing more than my fulfillment,
> surrender to his will is increasingly possible.

The possibility that I will actually enjoy what God wants for me
is radically different from my own infant-believer understanding of
God's will. But it is a very biblical concept. The psalmist David wrote,
"Take delight in the LORD, and he will give you the desires of your
heart" (Psalm 37:4). My heart's desires, then, are from God. In fact, the
desires of my heart may actually reveal to me the will of God.

Looking back, I can see that God's hopes for me were not that I
be a missionary in the traditional sense that I understood it. God did
not want me to live overseas at all. In fact, God's will for me is completely congruous with my own needs and desires. I stay at home
and write. One day, as I was happily working on a new manuscript,
I found myself thanking God for this privilege. Then, in one of those
Spirit-whispered moments, I thought of the various translations of
my books. Through those translations, I have been in Africa, the
Middle East, Asia, Europe and South America, though I never became an overseas missionary.

My friends Ted and Lisa, on the other hand, have spent most of their lives ministering to churches in South America. And for them, as for me, God's will and their desires meshed perfectly together. In one letter Lisa wrote, "I can't believe that God has allowed us to be in such a beautiful place doing such wonderful things." All of this reflects the God who said to the people of Israel, "I know the plans I have for you . . . plans to prosper you and not to harm you, plans to give you hope and a future" (Jeremiah 29:11 NIV). God's plans for us are good ones.

LISTENING AS OTHERS DISCERN GOD'S WILL

Group spiritual direction is a wonderful place for us to support and help each other discern God's good desires for us. When we meet we can ask questions of one another to help clarify what the desires of our hearts really are. Then in the process of group discussion we discover ways that those desires can be experienced in the context of a faithful relationship with God our Father. We provide a place to share our feelings and desires with several friends. But once again, the spiritual direction environment is unique. We are not used to this kind of dialogue. In order for the conversations in group direction to be transformational and healing, the friends in the group need to temporarily set aside their own feelings and interpretations in order to listen well. Sometimes this is hard to do.

When it was Nathan's turn to present in his group, he decided to talk about a recent time of discernment. Even though he had already decided what he was going to do, he thought it would help him to describe the process to the group. He had been trying to decide whether or not to go on a church mission trip. He wanted to go, but it would mean leaving his wife and two children alone at home for several weeks. He felt torn between his desire to go, the needs of the mission and the desire to be with his family at a time when they needed him. It was not an easy decision. By the time he came to the group, he had decided to stay home. He shared about the opportunity he had received to go, why he wanted to go and why he wanted to stay home. He expressed his relief that he had chosen to stay home with his family.

Erin was the first person to respond to Nathan. "Oh!" she said, "You must feel so sad about not going!" Then she commented on how difficult it is for her to choose not to do something. The facilitator of the group noticed that Erin's response was not really in keeping with the feelings Nathan had expressed. She gently turned the group back by asking Nathan, "Is that what you felt?" "No," he said. "I was relieved. By the time I made the decision, I felt so good to know that God would be with me and my family no matter what I decided. But I'm very glad I decided to stay home."

Nathan and Erin's experience in this group is not unusual. We all bring our own perspectives to the group. If Erin had been presenting, the group could have responded to the sadness she was expressing. But because it was Nathan's turn, the facilitator needed to return the group to what he was saying. By doing that, the group was able to celebrate with Nathan his sense of God's presence and guidance. This is what group spiritual direction is all about.

Nathan's choice was especially difficult because he really wanted to do two things at once. But many times the struggle is that we *want* to do one thing but we think we *should* do another. Group spiritual direction can be especially helpful in this predicament. In conversation with caring friends, we can talk about the "wants" and the "shoulds" in our lives. Sometimes the discernment process leads us to embrace something we would not choose. Sometimes we experience very unpleasant circumstances which we cannot change. Sometimes God himself seems to withhold peace and joy, and we experience what St. John of the Cross called the "dark night of the soul." Like Jesus in the Garden of Gethsemane, we may pray, "Father, if you are willing, remove this cup from me" (Luke 22:42).

At times like this, when it does not look like the boundary lines are in "pleasant places" (Psalm 16:6), our spiritual direction friends can help us. In human friendship, God enfleshes divine love. When God seems absent, our friends may remind us that God is still with us. When circumstances and relationships are difficult, we help each other *wait* to see God's love. In the welcoming, intimate circles of spiritual direction, we can process the aspects of discernment that are most difficult and most confusing. Like Nathan's friends in his spiritual direction group, we can offer to listen to one another, and to the desires of our own heart, with openness and love.

The Disposition of the Soul

Trust in God's love is another prerequisite for clarity in the discernment process. Participants in group spiritual direction can help one another in issues of discernment by encouraging each other to maintain an open, willing and waiting spirit. The person who is disposed to listen to God is a person who is open and surrendered. Mary, the mother of Jesus, demonstrated this kind of surrender. When the angel Gabriel appeared to Mary to tell her that she was going to have a baby—God's baby—she was not so sure. She questioned the angel. If I had been Mary, I would not only have asked how this could happen, I would also have questioned whether or not this was something I wanted to have happen to me. It would have taken quite a bit of convincing to bring me to surrender! But Mary ended up saying to Gabriel, "Behold, I am the handmaid of the Lord; let it be to me according to your word" (Luke 1:38 RSV). Mary's soul was willing, even if she didn't understand. That is the disposition of the soul that is ready for discernment: "Let it be to me according to your word." I suspect that many of our questions about the will of God would fade into the woodwork if we had that kind of openness.

A willing spirit is also a waiting spirit. Sometimes a good idea comes at the wrong time. I was in a group with a friend who struggled with whether or not to take on a large responsibility in her church. It seemed like a good fit with her gifts, but she didn't feel that she had time. Her conclusion after our time of listening and discussing was that if she had to decide right now, the answer would have to be no. Sometimes discernment means waiting for the right time. Friends may help us see that, and they can help us as we wait.

Waiting is often part of experiencing God's will. Sometimes we wait for opportunity. But sometimes what we really want is certainty, and certainty may not come until after the event. The reality of God's guidance is usually more evident with hindsight. When Moses pleaded for God's guidance and presence for the Israelites, God said to him, "While my glory passes by I will put you in a cleft of the rock, and I will cover you with my hand until I have passed by; then I will take away my hand, and you shall see my back; but my face shall not be seen" (Exodus 33:22-23). That has certainly been my experience with discernment. I pray for God's guidance, but then I'm more apt to see God's back than God's face. When the event, with all its questions, is over, I say to myself, *Oh, yes, God was there.* In group spiritual direction, our friends will wait with us, for the right time, until we can see that God has truly been with us.

DISCERNING BETWEEN THE TRUE SELF AND THE FALSE SELF
Perhaps most confusing of all in the process of discernment are the conflicting voices we hear within ourselves. Like Paul we say, "I can will what is right, but I cannot do it. For I do not do the good I want, but the evil I do not want is what I do" (Romans 7:18-19). Paul describes two minds within himself, one mind that wants to follow Christ, and one mind that is "a slave to the law of sin" (Romans 8:25). Another way to express how these two minds operate within us is to describe the false self and the true self. These two selves are described in the Bible in a variety of ways: the old man and the new

man, the sinful self and the redeemed self, the natural self and the transformed self. Calling these two parts of my inner being my "false self" and my "true self" has helped me probe more deeply into the spiritual reality of my life, and has helped me understand deeper levels of discernment.

The false self is all about the ego. The false self needs to impress others, needs approval, needs to be needed. When we're living according to our false self, we think that we're in control of our life and our world. We think that we're *entitled* to have all of our needs and desires met. We long for recognition. We are often lonely. We don't accept our limitations. We want to be independent and autonomous. We want to know everything and be sure that we are right.

The true self, on the other hand, knows that it is created by God in the image of the Creator, and yet is utterly unique. The true self knows that it is created to experience and express love. When we live according to our true self, we are free, limited only by God's love. We live in truth rather than under the illusions of the false self. We know that we are not in charge of life. We are God-centered rather than ego-centered. We manifest the fruits of the Holy Spirit— love, joy, peace, patience, kindness, generosity, faithfulness, gentleness and self-control (Galatians 5:22-23). In short, we live as though life is all about God and not about ourselves.

When Nathan was trying to decide whether or not he should go on the mission trip, the voices of his false self and true self contradicted each other. His false self wanted the public affirmation of doing missionary work. Staying at home with his family would be a more private choice. The false self wanted to accomplish something. The true self was willing to be present with his children even if it looked like nothing was happening. The false self wanted a break from family responsibilities. The true self was willing to persevere. These were things Nathan might have thought about as he made the decision.

On the other hand, someone else might have had a very different conversation about the same circumstances. The false self could have tried to convince the person making the choice that going on a mission trip would be a waste of time, compared with what could be done at his regular job. The false self could have said that God would never ask him to reach so far beyond his comfort zone. Or the false self could have reminded him that he would miss a very exciting play-off football game if he went. The true self, then, would have responded with a very different perspective. The problem is that it is often hard to tell whether the true self or the false self is influencing us. This is where our friends can help us. Through the dialogue of group spiritual direction we can often hear the values and inclinations of the true self more clearly.

Listening to the true self may be a countercultural experience. Many of us have families, jobs, even churches where the false self is affirmed. We want to look good, be successful, appear to be in control of our lives. Spiritual direction provides a safe place where we can admit our fears, illusions and insecurities. It provides a place where we can remember that the main purpose of our lives is not to look good but to love well. We remember, as we talk about our lives in this safe environment, that God is utterly trustworthy and that we don't have to constantly fend for ourselves. With these friends in spiritual direction, we can try out what it feels like to really trust God rather than the values and goals of the false self. The more we trust God, the more clearly we can discern God's desires for us.

Discernment Among Friends

Sharing the experience of discernment with friends, then, is a process of growing confidence in God, even while we live with the insecurities of our own limitations. It is a process where we choose to embrace the authenticity of our true self and resist the illusions of our false self. Among our spiritual direction friends we can grow and be more open and willing to receive God's goodness. Our friends help us notice and accept the longings of our hearts—which reflect the desires of God's heart for us.

12

TROUBLESHOOTING PROBLEMS IN GROUP SPIRITUAL DIRECTION

S tarting out in group spiritual direction is a little like the ancient Celts who set sail, not knowing exactly where they were going. In group direction we know that we want to journey together toward God. We have some tools, and we know how to sail the boat. But we don't know precisely where God will take us.

When I went for spiritual direction for the first time, I was a little nervous. I didn't know where this experience would take me. I had a lot of questions. When newcomers arrive for group spiritual direction, I see some of the same nervousness and questions on their faces. And even though I have led group spiritual direction for several years and have become a spiritual director myself, I feel a little wary, scared and nervous when I meet with a group or an individual for the first time. I guess it goes with the territory.

We can be kind toward ourselves about this. The spiritual journey is important, and it's good to take our involvement in our own journey and in someone else's journey very seriously. Sometimes it is a little scary. It helps to remember that this is not really all about us. It is not our job to fix or teach. God, after all, is the real spiritual director. And God is used to our imperfect attempts to love and serve others. For all of us, this is a journey. We do not "arrive." The journey continues, with God drawing the map.

We can, however, take steps to see that the ship is seaworthy. In group spiritual direction we face several risks—problems that might make our boats leak along the way. In this chapter we'll look at three of the most common difficulties in group direction: uneven attendance, unclear leadership and uninformed participation.

ATTENDANCE

The problem of uneven attendance is a difficult one. At the beginning of each session of group spiritual direction in our church, I always try to make it very clear how important regular attendance is. To my disappointment, people still miss meetings because of work, illness, travel, even concerts. Absenteeism is a problem which will probably never be resolved. However, many groups have found that it helps to meet biweekly rather than weekly. This allows for a little more space between meetings and may help participants attend regularly. Meeting once a month can also work, but then if someone can't make it to a meeting, too much time is missed in sharing lives with one another.

When someone in the group is frequently absent, the facilitator should check in with that person. Is the group what they were looking for? Would they prefer to stop coming? Would a group meeting at another time be better? Would personal spiritual direction suit the individual's schedule better? The important thing is that the facilitator address the problem of absenteeism in an inviting, affirming way, allowing the person to either confirm their commitment to the group or drop out if necessary.

LEADERSHIP

Unclear leadership can also be a problem. The facilitator of the group needs to understand the perspective of spiritual direction and be gifted to gently and clearly lead the group in that direction. Some people emphasize that the facilitator needs to be a trained spiritual director. This would be ideal, but it's not always possible. Furthermore, not all trained spiritual directors will be good group facilitators, nor will all people who are gifted to lead this kind of group be spiritual directors. It is essential, however, that the facilitator be thoroughly familiar with the spiritual direction process. If at all possible, the facilitator should also be meeting for individual direction with a spiritual director. If for some reason individual spiritual direction isn't possible for the facilitator, they should, at the very least, be well-read in the area of spiritual direction.

Facilitators whose groups seem to flourish are not only familiar with spiritual direction but also with good group dynamics. They are comfortable and not apologetic in their leadership. They keep track of the time and gently redirect conversations that are getting too lengthy or too far off-track. They make sure all participants feel free to share, and they're comfortable with times of silence. They keep the focus on contemplative listening—to God and to the person presenting as directee. They lead clearly but humbly, allowing the Holy Spirit to be the guide.

In churches that have several groups meeting for spiritual direction, it is good to have the group facilitators meet together to address any problems that arise. (They will, of course, want to honor the confidentiality of the groups.) The facilitators can help and support one another, or call in a trained spiritual director to give feedback and guidance.

GROUP PARTICIPATION

Finally, inappropriate group participation can be a problem. This

happens when group members frequently make too many suggestions, quote too much from the Bible or other favorite books, talk
too much themselves, or try to fix everyone else's problems. The author of Proverbs had this to say: "He who answers before listening—
/ that is his folly and his shame" (Proverbs 18:13 NIV). In group spiritual direction there is a serious risk that someone will answer before
listening. While we want to be kind and gentle with ourselves and
with others in learning the process of group direction, this problem
can't be ignored.

One way to address the need for informed and loving group participation is to give careful instruction before the group actually begins meeting. Sometimes an extended workshop is held before the
sessions of group spiritual direction start where spiritual direction is
described at length and guidelines for the groups are clearly given.
Other groups choose to spend the first one or two sessions together
reading about and discussing spiritual direction. I have included
suggestions for group discussion of this book in appendix three.

THE PROBLEM THAT MIGHT SINK THE BOAT

Every group faces risks that might diminish their group direction experience. Usually these risks need to be addressed by both the participants and the facilitator. The following is a list of questions that
groups might face, with suggestions for moving past the problem.

What happens when one person dominates the group?

This happened to my friend Lucy, who was participating in a group
that included Susan, a woman going through a very painful family relationship. Week after week Susan talked and cried her way
through the group's time together. Unfortunately, the facilitator
latched on to Susan's needs and allowed her to dominate. Lucy felt
cheated out of the opportunity for good group direction.

When this kind of situation develops, it is the responsibility of both the facilitator and the group participants to respond lovingly but firmly. In Lucy's group the facilitator needed to say, "Susan, we want to support you, but tonight we have agreed to allow someone else to present. Perhaps in two weeks we can come back and pursue your situation a little more. Would that be okay with you?" The group, then, needs to support the facilitator's leadership. Sometimes groups have a magnetic attraction to the person who vocalizes the most needs. The people in Susan's group needed to resist the temptation to invite her to share more than the group could handle. This is a very difficult situation for groups, but it is essential that groups maintain balanced listening, caring and support.

What happens when one person in the group assumes the role of solving problems or giving answers?

Again, the facilitator needs to take the lead with comments like, "That's a valid point, but we want to give Tom the opportunity to arrive at his own conclusions." Or "Tom, what do you think about that? Does it resonate with where you are in this?" Or "Tom, what feelings do you have about what John just said?"

This is also the responsibility of the members of the group. We all make mistakes. At one time or another, all of us have offered unwanted advice. But we need to remind ourselves that the person presenting came not to hear us, but to hear God. I have one extroverted friend who has learned to count to ten before she speaks. While this may be a bit extreme in group direction, it is certainly good to pause with our own thoughts before we plunge into verbalizing them.

What happens when some in the group want to dissolve the group, and others want to continue?

This calls for group discernment! Hopefully, the group will have decided ahead of time how long they plan to meet and members will be committed to that length of time. At the end of the time, members of the group can share their feelings and thoughts about continuing and decide whether or not to commit to another time period. In our church we met six to eight times each semester. The individual groups stayed the same during that time. In the fall and again in the winter we held introductory sessions where new people were invited to join. Then new groups were established. This arrangement worked well with the fluidity of church life. But in other situations groups may choose to meet for a year or longer. It is important to clarify these expectations before the group starts.

EVALUATION

Because problems can indeed "sink the ship," it's helpful to provide times for evaluation. For ongoing groups, evaluating after the first three meetings, and then again after a few months, is a good idea. The facilitator can select a few of the following questions to discuss during a brief time of evaluation, probably at the end of a regular session.

- How do you think we're doing in our experience of group spiritual direction?

- Are we meeting the needs you hoped would be met when you joined?

- How is this like what you expected? How is it different?

- How do you think the group is doing in supporting the leadership of our group?

- How are we doing with our listening and our questions? Are there changes we should make?

- Are we talking too much? Too little?

- Are we trying to fix one another's problems in an inappropriate way?

- Is there anything about our group that you would like to see changed?

Having regular times for evaluation gives group members the security of knowing that problems will not escalate. It also helps give a sense of responsibility to keep the group on track. We may be looking to God to guide our boat, but regular evaluations help us keep the sail set.

Remembering that this is a journey, we can take heart—even when problems arise—in knowing that God is with us, within each of us and present in all that happens. Group spiritual direction is a wonderful opportunity to travel together.

13

GETTING STARTED

One question frequently asked is, "How can I start a group for spiritual direction?" Because this ministry is just being rediscovered, this is an important question to address. How do I even begin, when no one else seems to know what I'm talking about? Sometimes there are only one or two people in a church who have even heard of spiritual direction. Group spiritual direction, where people share very personally about their spiritual journeys, may be an unusual experience. The following suggestions are my own effort to address this problem. Perhaps these ideas will trigger something for you and help you start a ministry of group spiritual direction among your own circle of friends.

Before you start, spend some time musing on what you'd really like. Would you like to meet in a church, in a home or someplace else? Would you like to meet during the day or in the evening? Would you be willing to lead the group or would you like someone else to facilitate? Do you want everyone to have the same theological perspective or would you like a variety? How often and for how long would you like to meet?

A next step is to survey the people you know who live on the growing edge of their own faith. See if three or four of them would be open to gathering together to explore group spiritual direction. Invite someone who has been in a spiritual direction group to talk with your group about the nature of this experience. If you can't find someone already familiar with spiritual direction, you and your friends could read this book together and discuss it as a group. After reading the book, you could commit to meeting for as many times as there are people in the group, allowing everyone to share once. You could take turns facilitating, or you could lead the group yourself. At the end of the initial commitment, evaluate and decide where you want to go from there.

Another way to begin is to look for a spiritual director in your area. Meet with that person yourself, by phone or in person, and see if you have a sense of connection. Ask the spiritual director if they would be willing to meet with you and three or four friends. Plan an introductory meeting where you can discuss expectations and see if it looks like the group will work well together.

You might also ask your pastor to gather a few people he or she knows in the congregation who might like group spiritual direction. Perhaps the pastor would even send out a letter, setting up a time for an introductory meeting. Even if the pastor cannot participate personally, he or she may be able to put you in touch with others who are interested. You could lead an informational time to tell people about spiritual direction and spiritual direction groups. Then you might ask if a few people would like to try to do this with you. Remember that you don't have to create the perfect group. If each person in the group is committed to grace and truth, and if each person longs to grow closer to God, the group will bear fruit.

Another possibility for initiating group spiritual direction is to ask a group you are already in (a Bible study or small group) if they would like to try this way of relating for about six times. Perhaps everyone in the group could read this book first. I know of one Bible study group who decided to alternate: one week for Bible study and one week for spiritual direction.

As you pray about the various possibilities for starting a group, one or two may begin to stand out to you. Pursue those ideas. If they don't work out, return to prayer. Perhaps something else will come along. This is not a program to be established but an opportunity to be received. Be open and creative. If a group does not work out, look for one other friend and suggest a two-person group.

Perhaps reading this book has prompted you to seek out personal spiritual direction. Ask around about finding a spiritual director in your area. Asking like-minded friends is one of the best ways to find a spiritual director. If you cannot find a spiritual director through a church or someone you know, you can go to the Seek and Find directory on the Spiritual Directors International website, located at www.sdiworld.org. Set up an initial interview with your potential spiritual director to ask questions of one another and see if you both feel it would be a good fit. Whatever you decide, proceed with faith and with confidence that God does not intend for us to journey alone. May God give you companions so that you can indeed seek God together.

APPENDIX 1

Suggested Format for Group Spiritual Direction

The following schedule is based on a one-hour meeting with five participants.

Gathering of participants—5 minutes

Opening time of quiet—15 minutes
Possibilities for this time include
- silence
- quiet music
- guided meditation, Scripture reading or spiritual reading

Brief check-in time—10 minutes
Each member shares for about 2 minutes from their own lives.

Group spiritual direction—30 minutes
Directee presents—10 minutes
Time of silence—2 minutes
Group responds and interacts with directee—15 minutes
Time of silent prayer for directee—2 minutes
Time for directee to debrief about how the experience felt—
1 minute

If the group is meeting for two hours, a second directee can present. Or the group may decide to have a longer response time to one directee.

APPENDIX 2

Guided Meditations and Other Beginnings

The opening few minutes of the group spiritual direction time will set the tone for the meeting. This beginning time is an opportunity for members of the group to settle down, release the cares of the day and turn the focus of their attention to God. Usually the facilitator leading the experience decides how to spend those opening minutes. A time of silence is one option, but for people who are inexperienced in being silent, this might be too much to ask. Therefore, in this appendix I suggest four different ways to begin the time of group direction: with music, lectio divina, the daily examen or guided meditation. All of these experiences include silence but also give gentle direction during the silence. Each suggestion is intended to give the individuals in the group an opportunity to reflect on their own lives and their relationship with God. This time will help them enter into the communal experience of seeking God with one another and, hopefully, will allow each person to release the demands of their personal lives in order to prepare for the time of focusing on God's interaction with one person in the group.

MUSIC

Quiet, reflective music is a good way to help people transition into the group spiritual direction experience. There are many recorded pieces to choose from. I like to use vocal music that includes Scripture. John Michael Talbot and Monica Brown are two artists who do this well. John Michael Talbot's music is available through Christian bookstores and on Amazon. Monica Brown's CDs can be ordered through her website, www.emmausproductions.com. Both of these artists have songs that are almost entirely Scripture. Sometimes I combine a song with a reading of the Scripture passage. Talbot's song "I Am the Vine," for example, works well with a reading from John 15. Monica Brown's CD *Holy Ground* also has a number of pieces based on Scripture.

You can also use nonvocal music to begin your group direction experience. My musician friends have told me that it's better to use music that isn't too familiar. Music from well-known classical pieces, they said, were distracting rather than quieting. Michael Hoppe is a composer and artist whose CDs have worked well for us. His work is widely available in the secular market and on Amazon.

Quiet music can be used on its own at the start of your time together, or it can be combined with one of the following meditative experiences.

Lectio Divina

Lectio divina ("spiritual reading," see chapter seven) is one good way to begin group spiritual direction. It starts with a time of silence, followed by the facilitator reading a short passage of Scripture very slowly. After another moment of silence, the verse or passage can be read again. Then participants are encouraged to spend several minutes in silence reflecting on the word, thought or feeling that came to their attention while the Scripture was read. The facilitator may want to close the time by suggesting that participants see if they sense any invitation from God in their reflection on the passage. Or the facilitator may simply read the passage again and close with a brief prayer.

There are, of course, many passages of Scripture which could be used for the experience. Here are three that would work well.

Psalm 1:3: "They are like trees planted by streams of water, which yield their fruit in its season, and their leaves do not wither. In all that they do, they prosper."

Lamentations 3:22-24: "The steadfast love of the Lord never ceases, his mercies never come to an end; they are new every morning; great is your faithfulness. 'The Lord is my portion,' says my soul, 'therefore I will hope in him.'"

Matthew 11:28-30: "Come to me, all you that are weary and are carrying heavy burdens, and I will give you rest. Take my yoke upon you, and learn from me; for I am gentle and humble in heart, and you will find rest for your souls. For my yoke is easy, and my burden is light."

There are many ways to close this time of lectio. A brief spontaneous prayer from the facilitator works well. If a written prayer is preferred, one good source is *The HarperCollins Book of Prayers,* compiled by Robert Van de Weyer. This collection includes prayers from many great Christian teachers and authors.

The Daily Examen

Allowing time for participants to practice the daily examen (chapter nine) is another good way to use the opening minutes of group spiritual direction. Again, the facilitator begins this experience with a minute or two of silence. Then the facilitator may ask the following questions, allowing participants to reflect on each question for about two minutes.

1. When today did you feel the most joy, the most freedom or the most loved? In other words, at what time (or times) today were you most aware of the presence of God?

2. When today were you least aware of the presence of God, or when did you feel the least loved, the least free or the most discouraged?

3. As you reflect on these moments in your day, what prayer rises up in your heart?

Then the facilitator may lead into the time of group direction with a prayer. This prayer from the psalmist lends itself well to this setting: "Let the words of my mouth and the meditation of my heart be acceptable to you, O LORD, my rock and my redeemer" (Psalm 19:14).

Both lectio divina and the daily examen could be followed by a time of very brief feedback from those participants who would like to verbalize their reflections with the group. This should be limited to one or two sentences from anyone who wants to speak. This opening time can also remain personal and private without group sharing. The group, under the guidance of the facilitator, can decide what works best for them.

GUIDED MEDITATIONS

In our church, guided meditations work well as a way to begin group spiritual direction, as most of the people in our groups are comfortable with the Bible and have some familiarity with applying the truths of Scripture to their own lives. The meditations are not Bible study, however, nor are the questions discussed as we go along. The questions, rather, allow each member of the group to enter into a passage of Scripture and focus on how that passage might reflect some way God is at work in their own lives. Reflecting on their own lives and turning their attention to God helps participants let go of the cares and struggles they bring into the session. This allows them to focus more clearly on the directee when we move into the time of group direction.

I have included five meditations which could be used at the beginning of your group spiritual direction time. Each meditation includes a time for quiet, followed by a Scripture reading and then a series of questions. The symbol ++++ after the questions indicates a pause of about a minute to give time for personal reflection. The Scripture is read and the questions asked by the facilitator. Some participants might choose to write out their reflections in a journal. Others may want to respond quietly without writing anything down.

The following five meditations are specifically designed to be used in the opening fifteen minutes of group spiritual direction, but other printed materials could be adapted for this time. (A good resource is *The Spiritual Formation Bible,* edited by Timothy Jones and published by Zondervan, which includes thoughtful, meditative questions in the margins, next to the biblical text.) Also note that these meditations are not intended for discussion, although some groups may decide to include a time for limited personal response to the meditation experience.

Meditation 1
James 1:5
Generous Wisdom

1. As you settle down into the quiet of this meditation, think of an area in your life where you have a special longing for wisdom. Be quiet for a few minutes, letting go of the cares of your day, and turning your attention to God. (Note to leader: Be sure to give ample time for this. We have a tendency to want to fill silence, but this time of quiet is important.)

2. Listen to the Word of the Lord:

   If any of you is lacking in wisdom, ask God, who gives to all generously and ungrudgingly, and it will be given you.

3. Tell God in prayer about the area of your life where you would like wisdom. What's happening in that situation or relationship? In what ways do you feel you need wisdom? ++++ God gives generously. Think of a time when someone shared generously with you. How did you feel? ++++ How do you experience God's generosity? ++++ God also gives "ungrudgingly." Think of a time when you experienced someone giving grudgingly. How did you feel? ++++ When might you worry that God is responding to your prayers in a grudging or ungenerous way? ++++ Another Bible translation says that God gives wisdom "without finding fault" (NIV). Spend some time reflecting on the fact that God does not find fault with you in your request for wisdom. ++++ What word or idea from this verse do you want to take with you into your week?

Meditation 2
Luke 2:25-32, 36-38
Waiting with Simeon and Anna

1. Take a minute or two to get settled. Breathe deeply. Reflect briefly on your day and then exhale one more time, releasing the cares and burdens you are carrying with you. Turn your attention to the love God is extending to you.

2. Listen to the account of Simeon and Anna that takes place when Mary and Joseph bring Jesus to the temple according to the law of the Lord.

> Now there was a man in Jerusalem whose name was Simeon; this man was righteous and devout, looking forward to the consolation of Israel, and the Holy Spirit rested on him. It had been revealed to him by the Holy Spirit that he would not see death before he had seen the Lord's Messiah. Guided by the Spirit, Simeon came into the temple; and when the parents brought in the child Jesus, to do for him what was customary under the law, Simeon took him in his arms and praised God, saying,
>
>> Master, now you are dismissing your servant in peace,
>>   according to your word;
>> for my eyes have seen your salvation,
>>   which you have prepared in the presence of all peoples,
>> a light for revelation to the Gentiles
>>   and for glory to your people Israel.

Luke also tells us about Anna.

> There was also a prophet, Anna the daughter of Phanuel, of the tribe of Asher. She was of a great age, having lived with her husband seven years after her marriage, then as a widow to the age of eighty-four. She never left the temple but wor-

shiped there with fasting and prayer night and day. At that
moment she came, and began to praise God and to speak
about the child to all who were looking for the redemption
of Jerusalem.

3. Take a few minutes to respond to Simeon's and Anna's experiences of waiting. Put yourself in one of their places and think
about what the waiting might have felt like. ++++ What is something you've been waiting for for a long, long time? ++++ What are
some of your thoughts and feelings as you're waiting? ++++ If you
had to wait for decades, as Simeon and Anna did, how would you
feel about that? ++++ Luke said that the Holy Spirit "rested" upon
Simeon. Take a minute or two to reflect on the Holy Spirit being
with you in your waiting. What difference does that make for you?
++++ The Holy Spirit revealed truth to Simeon and Anna. How do
you experience the Holy Spirit's comfort and truth in your own
life? ++++ Take another minute or two to pay attention to any way
the Spirit is at work in you as you're waiting right now.

Meditation 3
Exodus 5:7-9
Bricks Without Straw

1. As you turn your attention toward God, you might want to sit quietly with your hands open and turned downward. Take a minute or two and use your hands as a symbol of letting go of your desires for control, affirmation and security. Now turn your hands upward as a symbol of your desire to receive whatever God wants to give you during this time. Sit quietly, waiting to hear the Word of the Lord.

2. The Old Testament account of the Israelites' slavery in Egypt includes a very gripping story of the time Moses asked Pharaoh for permission to spend three days of worship in the wilderness. Instead of granting the request, Pharaoh accused the Israelites of being lazy and said to their supervisors,

   > You shall no longer give the people straw to make bricks, as before; let them go and gather straw for themselves. But you shall require of them the same quantity of bricks as they have made previously; do not diminish it, for they are lazy; that is why they cry, "Let us go and offer sacrifice to our God." Let heavier work be laid on them; then they will labor at it and pay no attention to deceptive words.

3. Picture yourself as an Israelite slave in these circumstances. You're tired and weary and now this additional work has been put on you. How do you feel? ++++ Consider the circumstances and relationships of your life at this time and see if there are places where you're asked to do more than you think you can do. In what ways is your situation similar to or different from what the Israelites experienced? ++++ Does someone else think you're lazy? Do you accuse yourself of being lazy? ++++ How do you feel about not be-

ing able to do all that you think you should do in this situation or relationship? ++++ Who acts like Pharaoh in your own life? God? Yourself? Someone else? ++++ Paul wrote to the Christians in Galatia, "You are no longer a slave but a child, and if a child then also an heir, through God" (Galatians 4:7). Remembering your own situation, in what ways do you feel like a slave and in what ways do you feel like a child-heir? ++++ Notice any quiet comfort or guidance God wants to communicate to you. Be still with that invitation.

Meditation 4
Luke 19:1-10
Jesus and Zacchaeus

1. Sit comfortably and quietly for a minute or two. Breathe deeply. Try to let go of the anxieties of your day. Focus your attention on the Spirit of God living within you.

2. Now listen to the account of Jesus and Zacchaeus:

   [Jesus] entered Jericho and was passing through it. A man was there named Zacchaeus; he was a chief tax collector and was rich. He was trying to see who Jesus was, but on account of the crowd he could not, because he was short in stature. So he ran ahead and climbed a sycamore tree to see him, because he was going to pass that way. When Jesus came to the place, he looked up and said to him, "Zacchaeus, hurry and come down; for I must stay at your house today." So he hurried down and was happy to welcome him. All who saw it began to grumble and said, "He has gone to be the guest of one who is a sinner." Zacchaeus stood there and said to the Lord, "Look, half of my possessions, Lord, I will give to the poor; and if I have defrauded anyone of anything, I will pay back four times as much." Then Jesus said to him, "Today salvation has come to this house, because he too is a son of Abraham. For the Son of Man came to seek out and to save the lost."

3. Spend a few minutes reflecting on how you might have experienced a similar encounter with Jesus. In your imagination picture a place you go to often (your home, your office, your neighborhood, any spot that you frequent). Imagine yourself looking in on whatever is happening there, as Zacchaeus looked down from the tree in Jericho. ++++ Who do you see in your picture? What

are they doing or talking about? ++++ Picture Jesus entering the scene. What does Jesus do or say? ++++ Now gently enter the room or place you're picturing in your imagination. How do you feel about being there? ++++ Is there anything you want to ask Jesus about what's going on? ++++ What does Jesus say to you? ++++ How do the people around you respond to your conversation with Jesus? Do they grumble about it as Zacchaeus's friends did or do they encourage you? ++++ If Jesus said he wanted to engage in your life today (as he did with Zacchaeus), how might you expect to encounter him?

Meditation 5
1 Kings 19:11-13
Listening for God

1. Be still and prepare to listen to God. Acknowledge your desire to listen. As much as you can, let go of the distractions of the day that might interfere with listening. Breathe deeply and welcome the Holy Spirit into your inner being.

2. Listen to the account of Elijah, God's prophet, who was running from Jezebel and longing to hear God speak to him.

   [An angel] said, "Go out and stand on the mountain before the LORD, for the LORD is about to pass by." Now there was a great wind, so strong that it was splitting mountains and breaking rocks in pieces before the LORD, but the LORD was not in the wind; and after the wind an earthquake, but the LORD was not in the earthquake; and after the earthquake a fire, but the LORD was not in the fire; and after the fire a sound of sheer silence. When Elijah heard it, he wrapped his face in his mantle and went out and stood at the entrance of the cave. Then there came a voice to him that said, "What are you doing here, Elijah?"

3. Spend some time in quiet reflection on how God communicates with you. In your own life, what circumstances, relationships or ideas seem like great winds or earthquakes? ++++ Which parts of your life make the most noise? ++++ Which parts of your life consume you, as a fire consumes anything in its path? ++++ Spend a few minutes reflecting on the "sound of sheer silence." What would that be like for you? ++++ Other Bible translations say Elijah heard the gentle whisper of God (NIV). What would it be like to hear God's gentle whisper? ++++ If God said to you, "What are you doing here?" how would you

answer? ++++ Spend some time listening to the "sheer silence" or the "gentle whisper" of God. If you'd like, try to put whatever you hear in words. Or you may prefer to sit in silence in the presence of God.

APPENDIX 3

Discussion Guide for *Seeking God Together*

The series of questions here is designed to provide content for a group discussion of ninety minutes or so on the content of the whole book. It is divided into three major topical sections. Feel free to select and adapt the questions here to suit your group's interests.

DEFINING GROUP SPIRITUAL DIRECTION

1. How would you describe spiritual direction to someone who has never heard of it? How do you think individual spiritual direction might be helpful on the spiritual journey? What questions do you have about spiritual direction?

2. Spiritual direction groups are different from other church experiences. How does group direction sound different from some of your own experiences in small groups?

3. The author says that spiritual direction helps people "grow in their faith, love others more fully and participate in the mission of the church more effectively." How do you think group spiritual direction might help people be more effectively engaged in the mission of the church?

Practicing Spiritual Direction

4. As you reflect on your own experiences of *being listened to,* how do you like someone to listen to you? What do you not like?

5. The author says that "good questions give life to the process of group spiritual direction." In what ways do you think this might be true? How do you feel when someone asks you a question about your spiritual journey? How do you feel about asking someone else a question about his or her spiritual journey?

6. Are you more comfortable processing your thoughts or your feelings? What is your response to the author's conclusion that the heart, spiritually speaking, includes both thoughts and feelings?

Engaging in the Spiritual Journey

7. Describe a time in your life when you experienced informational reading of the Bible. Describe a time when you experienced transformational reading of the Bible.

8. What is the predominant understanding of sin in your own Christian circles? How is this similar to or dissimilar from the author's perspective that sin is believing lies rather than believing God?

9. Which image works best for you in describing your own prayer life: the prodigal son coming home to the father, sailors in a boat with God at the helm, or two friends talking and listening to each other?

10. What is something about your temperamental preferences that you would like people to know about you? In what ways is this preference affirmed or not affirmed by others?

11. Describe a time in your own life when you needed to make a difficult decision. How did your close friends help or not help you in the process?

12. If you decide to participate in group spiritual direction, what hopes do you have for the experience? What fears do you have?

SUGGESTED READING

CHAPTER 1: A FIRST LOOK AT SPIRITUAL DIRECTION

Benner, David. *Sacred Companions*. Downers Grove, Ill.: InterVarsity Press, 2002.

Fryling, Alice. *The Art of Spiritual Listening*. Colorado Springs: Shaw Books, 2003.

Guenther, Margaret. *Holy Listening*. Cambridge, Mass.: Cowley Publications, 1992.

CHAPTER 2: COMPANIONS ON THE JOURNEY

Bakke, Jeanette. *Holy Invitations*. Grand Rapids: Baker Books, 2000.

Hendricks, Patricia. *Hungry Souls, Holy Companions*. Harrisburg, Penn.: Morehouse Publishing, 2006. This one is specifically focused on spiritual direction for young people.

Merton, Thomas. *Spiritual Direction and Meditation*. Collegeville, Minn.: Liturgical Press, 1960.

CHAPTER 3: GROUP SPIRITUAL DIRECTION

Dougherty, Rose Mary. *Group Spiritual Direction*. Mahwah, N.J.: Paulist Press, 1995.

Dougherty, Rose Mary, ed. *The Lived Experience of Group Spiritual*

Direction. Mahwah, N.J.: Paulist Press, 2003.

CHAPTER 4: THE POWER OF LISTENING

Nouwen, Henri. *Spiritual Direction: Wisdom for the Long Walk of Faith.*
New York: HarperSanFrancisco, 2006.
Palmer, Parker J. *Hidden Wholeness.* San Francisco: Jossey-Bass,
2004.

CHAPTER 5: ASKING LIFE-GIVING QUESTIONS

Caliguire, Mindy. *Discovering Soul Care.* Soul Care® Resources.
Downers Grove, Ill.: IVP Connect, 2007.
Stairs, Jean. *Listening for the Soul: Pastoral Care and Spiritual Direction.*
Minneapolis: Augsburg, 2000.

CHAPTER 6: EXPLORING THOUGHTS AND FEELINGS

Linn, Dennis, Sheila Fabricant Linn and Matthew Linn. *Healing the
Purpose of Your Life.* Mahwah, N.J.: Paulist Press, 1999.
Nouwen, Henri. *The Way of the Heart.* New York: Ballantine Books,
1981.

CHAPTER 7: MEDITATING ON SCRIPTURE TOGETHER

Hall, Thelma. *Too Deep for Words.* Mahwah, N.J.: Paulist Press,
1988.
Mulholland, M. Robert, Jr. *Shaped by the Word.* Nashville: Upper
Room, 1985.

CHAPTER 8: SIN, CONVICTION AND CONFESSION

May, Gerald. *Addiction and Grace.*: San Francisco: Harper and Row,
1988.
———. *The Dark Night of the Soul.* New York: HarperSanFrancisco,
2004.

Chapter 9: Sharing the Journey of Prayer

Barton, Ruth Haley. *Invitation to Solitude and Silence*. Downers Grove, Ill.: InterVarsity Press, 2004.

Keating, Thomas. *Intimacy with God*. New York: Crossroad, 1994.

————. *Open Mind, Open Heart*. New York: Continuum, 1986.

Chapter 10: Temperament and How We Communicate

Benner, David. *The Gift of Being Yourself*. Downers Grove, Ill.: InterVarsity Press, 2004.

Hirsh, Sandra Krebs, and Jane A. G. Kise. *Soul Types*. New York: Hyperion, 1998.

Tieger, Paul D., and Barbara Barron-Tieger. *Do What You Are*. Boston: Little, Brown, 1992.

Chapter 11: Discernment Among Friends

Green, Thomas H. *Weeds Among Wheat*. Notre Dame, Ind.: Ave Maria Press, 1984.

Hougen, Judith. *Transformed into Fire: An Invitation to Life in the True Self*. Grand Rapids: Kregel, 2002.

NOTES

Chapter 2: Companions on the Journey

page 15   The poet John Milton: John Milton, *Tetrachordon*, 1645.

page 16   "reflects the essence": Gerald G. May, *Care of Mind, Care of Spirit* (New York: HarperSanFrancisco, 1992), p. 7.

page 17   "had a profound appreciation": Gerald G. May, *The Dark Night of the Soul* (New York: HarperSanFrancisco, 2004), pp. 66-67.

page 17   "soul is not a separate part": Ibid., p. 42.

page 18   "the soul is like a wild animal": Parker Palmer, *A Hidden Wholeness* (San Francisco: Jossey-Bass, 2004), p. 58.

page 19   "midwives for the soul": Margaret Guenther, *Holy Listening* (Cambridge, Mass.: Cowley Publications, 1992), p. 85.

pages 19-20   "Being a spiritual friend": Tilden Edwards, *Spiritual Friend* (New York: Paulist Press, 1980), p. 125.

page 20   "The focus of this kind": William A. Barry and William J. Connolly, *The Practice of Spiritual Direction* (New York: HarperSanFrancisco, 1986), pp. 6, 7.

page 21   "The whole purpose of spiritual direction": Thomas Merton, *Spiritual Direction and Meditation* (Collegeville, Minn.: Liturgical Press, 1960), p. 16.

page 21   "we know that the last thing": Palmer, *Hidden Wholeness,* pp. 58-59.

Chapter 3: Group Spiritual Direction

page 27   "a process of being conformed": M. Robert Mulholland Jr., *An Invitation to a Journey* (Downers Grove, Ill.: InterVarsity Press, 1993), p. 12.

Chapter 4: The Power of Listening

page 40   It also means to view (a person or object): *Random House College Dictionary*, rev. ed., s.v. "contemplate."

page 41   "This kind of listening": Kenneth Blue, *Authority to Heal* (Downers Grove, Ill.: InterVarsity Press, 1987), p. 128.

page 41   "Intense listening is indistinguishable": Ibid.

page 41   "the greatest gift I could give": Margaret Guenther, *Holy Listening* (Cambridge, Mass.: Cowley Publications, 1992), p. 94.

Chapter 5: Asking Life-Giving Questions

page 45   "What needs to be said is": Henri Nouwen, *Spiritual Direction: Wisdom for the Long Walk of Faith* (New York: HarperSanFrancisco, 2006), p. 9.

pages 45-46   "You seek answers": Ibid., p. 11.

page 46   "In the ministry of spiritual direction": Margaret Guenther, *Holy Listening* (Cambridge, Mass.: Cowley Publications, 1992), p. 65.

Chapter 6: Exploring Thoughts and Feelings

page 56   "the intellect, memory, emotions": Leland Ryken, James C. Wilhoit and Tremper Longman III, eds., *Dictionary of Biblical Imagery* (Downers Grove, Ill.: InterVarsity Press, 1998), p. 368.

Chapter 7: Meditating on Scripture Together

page 66   "We seek to master": M. Robert Mulholland Jr., *Shaped by the Word* (Nashville: Upper Room, 1985), p. 50.

page 66   "allow the text": Ibid., p. 54.

pages 67-68   "Repetition is the soul": Michael Casey, *Sacred Reading* (Liguori, Mo.: Triumph Books, 1996), pp. 24, 31.

page 68   "lectio divina is an element": Ibid., p. 9.

pages 68-69   "He began to find himself": Margaret Silf, *Inner Compass* (Chicago: Loyola Press, 1999), p. xxi.

page 69   "When you have to listen to abuse": Thomas C. Oden and Christopher A. Hall, *Mark*, Ancient Christian Commentary on Scripture, ed. Thomas C. Oden (Downers Grove, Ill.: InterVarsity Press, 1998), p. 65.

Chapter 9: Sharing the Journey of Prayer

page 87   "true, whole prayer": Quoted in Richard Foster, *Prayer* (New York: HarperSanFrancisco, 1992), p. 1.

page 87   "prayer is not just dialogue": Michael Casey, *Toward God* (Liguori, Mo.: Triumph Books, 1995), p. 51.

page 88   "the key in all of our Scripture praying": Calvin Miller, *The Path of Celtic Prayer* (Downers Grove, Ill.: InterVarsity Press, 2007), p. 54.

page 90   "When the wind died": Ibid., p. 74.

pages 90-92   Thomas Keating, well known for his teaching: Cynthia Bourgeault expands on Keating's teaching in *Centering Prayer and Inner Awakening* (Cambridge, Mass.: Cowley Publications, 2004).

page 92   Walter Wangerin says: Walter Wangerin, *Whole Prayer* (Grand Rapids: Zondervan, 1998), p. 29.

page 94   "Then the monks were filled with joy": Calvin Miller, *Path of Celtic Prayer,* p. 82.

Chapter 10: Temperament and How We Communicate

page 103   In his *Institutes of the Christian Religion:* John Calvin, *Institutes of the Christian Religon,* ed. John T. McNeill, trans. Ford Lewis Battles (Louisville, Ky.: Westminster John Knox, 1960), p. 35.

page 104   "Each of the Redeemed": C. S. Lewis, *The Problem of Pain* (New York: Macmillan, 1962), p. 150.

Chapter 11: Discernment Among Friends

page 108   "one leading to fullness of life": David Lonsdale, *Listening to the Music of the Spirit* (Notre Dame, Ind.: Ave Maria Press, 1992), p. 51.

page 108   "one of the gifts": Ibid., p. 54.

page 108   discernment is always "tentative": Thomas H. Green, *Weeds Among the Wheat* (Notre Dame, Ind.: Ave Maria Press, 1984), p. 66.

page 109   "the God of the Judaeo-Christian tradition": Ibid., p. 33.

page 111   "Ignatius of Loyola suggests": David Benner, *Sacred Companions* (Downers Grove, Ill.: InterVarsity Press, 2002), p. 39.